# THE CHRISTIAN RIGHT IN REPUBLICAN STATE POLITICS

# THE CHRISTIAN RIGHT IN REPUBLICAN STATE POLITICS

Kimberly H. Conger

palgrave
macmillan

First published in 2009 by PALGRAVE MACMILLAN® in the United States—a division of St. Martin's Press LLC, 175 Fifth Avenue, New York, NY 10010.

Where this book is distributed in the UK, Europe and the rest of the world, this is by Palgrave Macmillan, a division of Macmillan Publishers Limited, registered in England, company number 785998, of Houndmills, Basingstoke, Hampshire RG21 6XS.

Palgrave Macmillan is the global academic imprint of the above companies and has companies and representatives throughout the world.

Palgrave® and Macmillan® are registered trademarks in the United States, the United Kingdom, Europe and other countries.

ISBN: 978-0-230-62079-7

Library of Congress Cataloging-in-Publication Data

Conger, Kimberly H.
   The Christian right in Republican state politics / Kimberly H. Conger.
      p. cm.
   Includes bibliographical references and index.
   ISBN 978-0-230-62079-7 (alk. paper)
   1. Republican Party (U.S.: 1854– ) 2. Christian conservatism—United States—States. 3. Christianity and politics—United States—States. 4. Christians—United States—States—Political activity. 5. U.S. states—Politics and government. I. Title.

JK2356.C65 2010
324.2734—dc22                                           2009013973

A catalogue record of the book is available from the British Library.

Design by Scribe Inc.

First edition: November 2009

10 9 8 7 6 5 4 3 2 1

Printed in the United States of America.

For Michael

# CONTENTS

# Tables

# Acknowledgments

Writing a book requires a scholar to incur many debts, intellectual and otherwise. But for a book like this, where the data and conclusions are built on the ideas, opinions, and emotions of a wide variety of people who are involved the political process, my greatest debt of gratitude has to be to the many political activists and observers who freely gave of their time and words, confidentially and with no incentive of repayment, to help me understand the strategy and success of the Christian Right in a number of states throughout the country. Without these individuals, this book would simply not exist.

I am also very fortunate to have good colleagues, both at Iowa State University and in the larger political science discipline, who have given me the gift of their time and thoughts on all or parts of this book in many different versions. John Green deserves my warmest appreciation. He read the manuscript at least twice all the way through, and it is much better for both his criticisms and encouragement. I would also like to thank Kathleen Cunningham, Lyman Kellstedt, Christopher Mooney, Matthew Potoski, Rebecca Sager, and David Walls for reading and commenting on various chapters of the manuscript. Since this book began, many versions ago, as a dissertation, I would especially like to thank the members of my dissertation committee, Paul Allen Beck, Herbert Weisberg, and Kira Sanbonmatsu.

The research contained in this book would not have been possible without the support and resources of the Political Science Department and Iowa State University as a whole. A special summer grant from the College of Liberal Arts and Sciences allowed me to travel to Arizona to do face to face interviews, and Political Science Department research monies allowed me to conduct research in Missouri and Indiana as well as fund other aspects of the research and writing of this book. I would also like to thank the graduate student Narren Brown and undergraduate students Nathan Chiaravalotti and John Burdine, who provided very able research assistance at various stages of this project.

My family has been a constant source of support and encouragement throughout the years of this project. My parents, in addition to instilling in me from an early age the desire to figure out the world around me, have for many years endured my pontifications with good-natured grace. Thank you for listening.

My husband, Michael, was present at the advent of the idea for this project and he has seen it through with more patience than I did. For his forbearance, eternal good humor, and most especially for his unfailing faith in me, I am inexpressibly grateful.

# CHAPTER 1

———◦✦◦———

## INTRODUCTION

### POLITICAL CONTEXT AND EVANGELICAL ACTIVISM

The fortunes of the Christian Right in American politics have ebbed and flowed in the several decades it has been a part of the political landscape. No sooner has a political pundit offered its obituary than it returns to the fray in some resurrected or reconstituted form. Periods of relative quiet have been followed by prolonged moments of activity and vociferousness. Thus, while the rhetoric of current political culture is one of studied inclusiveness and tolerance, seemingly precluding much of the movement's agenda, its basic political ideas, represented by organizations like the Family Research Council and Concerned Women for America, continue to guide the political choices of millions of voting Americans. It is for this reason, if no other, that we should continue to observe the evolving influence that the Christian Right exerts on American politics.

Perhaps the most tangible and enduring result of the presence of the Christian Right in the American political arena is the effect its influence has had on Republican politics at all levels. Like the persistence of the movement itself, the relative power the movement has enjoyed within the Republican Party has been debated with fervor by both scholars and journalists. Some suggest that the party has been "captured" by the Christian Right, while others cite the movement's divergence from the ideological mainstream as its primary drawback as a member of the Republican coalition. Most agree, however, that

the movement has become a permanent fixture in the calculations of Republican political strategists. Many believe that the
political mobilization of religious conservatives holds the key to
Republican victories at all levels of electoral contest.

The Christian Right first became active in the 1970s. They
mainly focused on the national level, concentrating on issues
from abortion to Christian Schools to the Strategic Defense
Initiative. The late 1980s and early 1990s signaled a shift in
Christian Right strategy; movement activists decided that
it was time to abandon the largely unsuccessful attempt to
influence federal policy and to move to the smaller and more
amenable arenas of the states and of grassroots politics. As
early as 1988, Pat Robertson was encouraging his rank and file
supporters to run for local offices themselves.[1] And by 1992,
Ralph Reed, then director of the Christian Coalition, was
claiming the takeover of the Republican Party to be the most
important goal for the pro-family movement. The *Los Angeles Times* noted at the time, "Reed's ultimate goal is to take
over the GOP from the bottom up. To do that, he can tap a
$10-million annual budget and call on dues-paying activists in
more than 100,000 born-again churches. This fall, more than
1,000 of these people were trained in the ways of taking over
precinct-level party committees, foreshadowing a larger effort
to dominate every state party organization."[2] The effects of
such a strategy were brought to fruition on a national level
in 1994 with the election of the first Republican Congress in
four decades. The strategy was also successful at more local
levels with the election of Christian Right supporters to many
local school boards and the introduction of referenda consistent with the movement's worldview.

Many have sought to link the "Republican Revolution" of
1994 to Christian Right activity on the national level along with
the movement's support of the Contract with America. But if
the influence so clear to political pundits on the national level had
a hand in the 1994 congressional elections, surely the movement
must also be influential at the state level. Congressional seats, at
least in their electoral milieu, are distinctly state offices. Thus the
Christian Right movement's activity at the state and local level

should not be underestimated. Statements by movement leaders themselves point to the importance of these arenas in the overall strategy of religious conservative political influence.

State-level politics provides fertile ground for the Christian Right. Because of the structure of American federalism and the devolution of regulatory power to the states, many of the issues taken up by state and local government are the types of social and family issues on which the movement thrives. Further, localized decision-making benefits a movement whose strength lies in grassroots mobilization. The Christian Right matters in state and local political contexts because it is a motivated minority, willing to pay attention to state and local issues and to educate its constituency on how to best pursue their policy goals. This can have a great impact in state and local politics as the movement and its supporters turn out in low interest elections and seek a voice in low profile issues. As is clear from even a casual attention to politics, the Christian Right concentrates its efforts on Republican politics; not just state-level parties, but also legislative and Congressional campaigns, ballot initiatives and referenda, and lobbying all branches of state and local government in support of their policy goals. Because of these traits, the Christian Right has demonstrated a growing impact on Republican politics in nearly every state over the past generation.

Perhaps most important, the movement will likely continue to thrive at the state level as national politics has become much less amenable with the advent of the Obama administration. The movement is set up for success in the states, as we will see throughout this book, and it seems likely that most activists will continue their state-level activity and influence even as the larger political discussion in the United States focuses mainly on economic issues. In fact, the current political realities at the national level, a Democratic president and Congress, and an electorate that seems ready and willing to give them the support and time they need to make lasting political changes, makes the subject of the Christian Right at the state level even more relevant. Because the arena of state politics is where we are most likely to see Christian Right activism over the next five or more years, understanding how the movement works, how it chooses political strategies, and what success it is likely to have is more important than political pundits yet realize.

Like all social movements, the power and importance of the Christian Right and its constituent organizations are highly dependent on the context in which its supporters find themselves. While some would argue that the Christian Right is not a social movement because of its members' middle-class and conservative characteristics, there is a growing acceptance among social movement scholars of the importance of such groups.[3] Further, the Christian Right displays the characteristics of classic social movements as they have been defined by observers and scholars. First, and most important, the Christian Right has a vision of itself as a threatened group.[4] Social movements use a group's perception of threat to mobilize activity and to give an explanation for its existence to both insiders and outsiders. Christian Right activists and supporters believe that the larger culture in the United States does not fit with their religious-moral views and that they are discriminated against because of these beliefs, particularly in the public policy arena, in speech and expression, and in entertainment options. The Christian Right is not a monolithic entity; it finds expression in numerous organizations and groups, fitting the description of a dispersed, multiheaded, and loosely coordinated social movement. Most importantly, though, there is a body of goals and policies that can be identified with the Christian Right even if not all are emphasized equally by these constituent organizations.

Though dispersed among a variety of political organizations, supporters of the Christian Right are certainly linked by nonpolitical means, which serve as mobilizing and efficacy-building situations. "The culture of evangelicalism encourages people to take political action, should they choose to. They are more likely to choose to do so if they know people who are active and if they can take action in ways that are religiously comfortable . . . [Their] agenda is set by the evangelical subculture, which thrives through an array of institutions that may not, on the surface, seem political . . . the evangelical subculture . . . is like a big ocean in which the Christian Right's activist fish swim and spawn."[5] This includes the personal transformations necessary to the cohesion of social movements. Christian Right participants are transformed from simply churchgoers into broadly involved political activists by their ongoing connection with other Christian Right participants and larger, frequently nonpolitical, organizations.

While it is true that the Christian Right has found its most obvious and enduring influence in state Republican politics, the movement's experiences in this arena have shaped its strategies and behavior as well. Each state's political context imposes a set of constraints on the movement and its ability to achieve its policy goals in that state. All fifty states have different laws and customs that govern political behavior and the creation of public policy. Thus the context in which the movement seeks political change is just as important as the movement itself when it comes to understanding how the movement operates and seeks power within a state's Republican politics. One of the most interesting developments in the life of the movement has been the degree to which Christian Right activists have become more sophisticated in their political strategies and behavior.[6] Much of this sophistication has come from learning the rules of the game in their particular state's politics and understanding how best to work within and around the constraints presented to them in their state context.

In examining the Christian Right in state-level Republican politics, we can see how important it is to understand both the movement itself and the context in which it operates. We need to understand not only that the movement matters in state politics, but also when, how, and why it matters. These are questions that can only be answered by examining both the Christian Right in its state-level incarnations and the state contexts in which the movement operates. Thus the basic research question for this project is, *How does state politics shape the Christian Right's strategy and affect its political success?*

In this book, I take a closer look at the Christian Right movement and its activities and successes at the state level. I offer a theory that explains how the movement interacts with the Republican Party and a state's political context and how movement influence and strategy is shaped by these interactions. Since each state has its own laws and practices, and each state movement has its own resources on which to draw, Christian Right activists have striven to learn how to operate in a variety of different contexts. My goal is to understand how the Christian Right operates within these real constraints of their state context. Moving beyond previous studies that seek to explain Christian Right influence, I take seriously the interaction between strategy and influence, and offer a way to observe how the political context in which the movement operates affects these singly and together. Exploring the Christian Right and its impact on American state politics helps explain how social movements go about trying to change public policy. In a larger sense, this also allows us to gain a more complete picture of group politics in general: how people come together to influence government and change the society in which they live. This book is an attempt to think systematically about these phenomena and put them into a framework that extends our understanding of politics and the activists who participate in it.

## ANALYTIC APPROACH

In order to understand the level of influence the Christian Right can achieve and how the movement chooses its political strategy based on the movement's internal resources and the state context in which activists find themselves, I follow earlier work in the study of the Christian Right, focusing on several states in an in-depth manner. This book moves beyond traditional case study work, however, in that it seeks generalizable understandings of Christian Right activities based on the evidence both from in-depth case studies of a few states and other data from a larger group of states.

A brief note on my use of terms is necessary. I use two terms in this book, which overlap but designate different conceptions of the movement. First, the term "Christian Right" is used to describe the religiously motivated social movement populated by activists and supporters. This social movement is made up of organizations and individuals who support a pro-family agenda including opposition to abortion, stem cell research, and gay marriage and support for local control of schools and tax policy that makes single-income families possible. This can mean members or supporters of Christian Right groups or unaffiliated individuals who are part of the larger network of information and political activity that characterizes the connections among different parts of the movement. Second, the term "religious conservatives" is used to denote the constituency of the Christian Right movement. These are primarily Evangelicals, but may be any other religiously motivated conservative individual who likely votes in ways consistent with Christian Right ideology and is a potential resource for movement mobilization. The bottom line is that the Christian Right is a social movement that is engaged in political action, while religious conservatives are those sympathetic to the movement, but not actively engaged in promoting the movement or its issues.

In order to investigate the relationship among state Christian Right movements and Republican politics, we must closely examine the dynamics of state politics and how the movement has sought influence in these contexts. There are several ways one can approach the relationship between the Christian Right movement and the Republican Party at the state level. One way is to look at the situation comprehensively, examining the relationship in every state. The other is to take a more idiographic approach, looking at the states individually, determining the specific conditions of the relationship in a particular state. The overarching goal is, in both cases, to not only explain the phenomenon in a particular state, but to identify regularities among states that will help us understand as a whole how the Christian Right interacts with Republican politics. Both of these approaches have their merits and both are utilized to some degree in this book, but the unique character of state politics suggests that the second approach may provide a more comprehensive view of the relationship between the party and the movement. Utilizing an idiographic approach in several states provides a comparison that allows me to draw higher level generalizations that can be tested across a wide variety of states. Thus we begin with case studies and move later to examine how those idiographic insights hold up against broader, more generalizable data.

Case studies allow me to make structured, focused comparisons among several states with the goal of both testing the proposed theory and examining the dynamics of the relationships among movement, party, and state politics.[7] Utilizing the case study method provides a wealth of information about how the Christian Right movement operates, how its leaders make strategic choices, how much influence the movement has, how the Republican Party is structured, and how the party responds to repel or integrate Christian Right activists. This information allows me to trace the process of Christian Right influence and determine how political opportunity structure, movement resources, and threat-based mobilization shape the strategy the movement chooses in order to advance its policy goals in state politics.

To this end, I have chosen three states on which to concentrate as I seek to explain how the Christian Right influences and shapes state politics and how the movement is, in turn, affected by the structure of the Republican Party and the larger political context in which it operates. The three states are Indiana, Missouri, and Arizona. I chose these particular states for several reasons. First, none of the states have been studied in depth by other scholars of the Christian Right movement. This is primarily the case because the states have not been considered to be ones that exhibited significant levels of movement influence.[8] Second, they are states that exhibit a moderate level of Christian Right influence in national studies and represent a variety of political cultures and religious traditions. Because the movement's experience in these states falls between complete success and failure, they represent the real battleground where the movement seeks influence and adapts to the political realities in each state. They are all also outside the South, where the movement has arguably had its greatest success and been the most studied. Third, it is also the case that each state has large and identifiable Evangelical communities that tend to facilitate Christian Right activism, successful or unsuccessful. So in these three states, I find the potential for painting a new picture of the state-level Christian Right movement, one that gives us a broad understanding of how the movement seeks power and policy change in existing political institutions. Ultimately, the states themselves are less important than the general understanding of the movement and its involvement in Republican politics that these states provide.

## Case Study Method

The case studies seek to tell the story of Christian Right influence during a period of time, drawing on history, laws, and personality to place that influence in proper context. Taking example from earlier case studies of Christian Right influence in the states,[9] from Fenno's[10] study of the "Home Style" of members of Congress, and other studies utilizing case methodology,[11] the case studies in this book draw from a wide variety of sources to present the comprehensive story of Christian Right influence in the Republican politics of these states.

While a good deal of the evidence comes from scholarly and public sources, a large portion of it is in the form of personal interviews conducted with political activists and observers in all three states over a period of several years. Each of the people I interviewed was promised complete confidentiality for their conversations with me. To give a brief idea of the scope of my data collection, I interviewed fifty-nine people in these three states. In Indiana, I interviewed sixteen people, four Christian Right activists, four Republicans, one Democrat, and seven journalists, academics, or political consultants. In Missouri, I interviewed twenty-one people, six Christian Right activists, two Republicans, two Democrats, and eleven journalists, academics, or political consultants. Finally, in Arizona, I interviewed twenty-two people, ten Christian Right activists, two Republicans, one Democrat, and nine people who were journalists, academics, or political consultants.

The interviews usually lasted between thirty to forty-five minutes. Participants were asked an overarching set of seven questions concerning their state's politics, its Christian Right movement, Republican Party, and the relationship between the two (see appendix A). In many cases participants volunteered valuable information not covered in the protocol. I also asked questions in each state that were specific to the state's political context. These were primarily based on the partisan distribution of the state's government, the laws that govern political parties and elections in the state, and state political issues of current controversy. Most of the interviews were done face to face, although some were phone interviews for the convenience of the participant. Most participants were referred to me by other interview participants. Using preexisting political and social contacts, I was able to identify a principal activist or politician within each state who was willing to introduce me to a variety of other potential interview participants. These contacts were, by far, more productive than the cold calling I did. In many ways, this could be considered a snowball sample where I was able to find a wide variety of participants by tapping into the social networks in Christian Right and Republican politics.

My primary approach to analysis of this information is thematic content analysis of the interviews; basically, I looked for the recurrent themes in the interviews I conducted. Events, issues, people, and evaluations that were consistently discussed by participants became the main concepts on which I focused. In many cases, participants addressed similar situations in diverse ways, adding to my understanding of the topic. Further, I sought to understand differences or inconsistencies in the narratives given by participants. Some inconsistencies appear to be disparity in the information available to participants; others, however, represent multiple explanations of a single situation, a finding that helps describe the ideological and social features of each state and illuminate its political situation.

The evidence on which I draw is comprised of these interviews plus publicly available data concerning the politics, personalities, and characteristics of the state, its politics and parties, the Christian Right movement, and the Evangelical community. While the non-interview data, particularly newspaper articles, allow me to assess the veracity of some of the interview data, much of the information gathered from these leaders is available in no other form. The perceptions, thoughts, and analyses of the interview participants provide a look into the mechanics of state politics and the motivations and strategies of both the Christian Right and the Republican Party it is trying to influence.

Beyond the three states on which I am concentrating, I have gathered evidence from all over the country through further interviews and publicly available information. In order to contextualize the relationship among Christian Right activists and state Republican politics, all together I have conducted over one hundred interviews in nine states with state Republican and Democratic party leaders, leaders of Christian Right political groups, members of both the political and religious media, political consultants of various partisan loyalties, and academic observers. These interviews allow me to gauge the motivations of Christian Right activists and catch a glimpse of the thought processes they used as they decided on the most effective strategy to achieve their policy goals all over the country.

In analyzing this qualitative data, I have primarily used process tracing to determine the decision making of Christian Right activists and a modified form of case study in order to understand the political constraints faced by the movement in each state. Process tracing is a way to identify the steps "in a causal process leading to the outcome of a given dependent variable of a particular case in a particular historical context."[12] Basically, it allows me to examine the causes of a nonrepeatable historical fact, like those examined in my case studies. Process tracing seeks the causal process, how and why a situation moves from A to B. Using extensive quotes from the political actors themselves, I am able to not only demonstrate how political contexts shape Christian Right strategy, but also to explain how movement activists react to these constraints and the process of seeking influence through them.

In order to follow the framework of a structured, focused comparison among these states, the case studies in this book all follow a similar pattern. First, I outline the general social and political context of each state, focusing particularly on those characteristics that have import for Christian Right influence. The case studies then detail the characteristics, history, and dynamics of the movement in each state. Next, the cases look at the relationship between the Christian Right movement and the Republican Party in each state, and at the relationship between the movement and legislative politics. This ordering allows a comparison among the states of how the political opportunity structure, movement resources, and threat mobilization interact to determine whether the movement works within or

around the Republican Party, or whether it goes home altogether. Finally, each case study concludes with an assessment of
how the case provides evidence, or not, for the theory.

## ROADMAP

In this introductory chapter, I have proposed the basic research
question for this project and laid out the analytical approach
for the remainder of the book. We have seen that the Christian
Right movement and its relationship with Republican politics
at the state level are impacted by the resources of the movement itself and by the state political context in which it occurs.
In order to understand this phenomenon more clearly, Chapter 2 begins by offering a brief history of the Christian Right
movement in the United States, particularly at the state level.
The second part of the chapter provides a review of the current
state of scholarly knowledge about the relationship among the
Christian Right and state Republican parties, and how social
movements and parties interact more generally. Chapter 3 lays
out my theoretical explanation for the variation in influence and
strategy of the Christian Right movement in state Republican
politics. First demonstrating why the Republican party is the
movement's primary goal for influence, the chapter focuses on
the threefold choice of the movement, to work within the party,
to work around it, or to go home.

In Chapters 4, 5, and 6, I offer in-depth case studies of the
relationship between the Christian Right and Republican politics in Indiana, Missouri, and Arizona. Following the theoretical
approach laid out in Chapter 3, I demonstrate how the Christian Right has chosen to work within or around the Republican
Party in each state, based on the political context in which activists find themselves. In Chapter 7, we turn to states in which the
Christian Right has chosen to "go home," to not seek influence
in state Republican politics.

Chapter 8 draws together the threads of analysis offered in
the case studies to examine more closely how these data fit my
theory. In it, I link the findings of the case studies together,
expand the analysis to a larger sample of states where the Christian Right's strategic choices can be determined from previous

research, and I more closely examine the relationship between influence and strategy. Finally, the conclusion of the book looks beyond the details of the story about the Christian Right movement and Republican politics—and the role of social movements in political parties—to show how this approach might help us understand other social movement/political party interactions.

The Christian Right is a long-term and powerful player in the Republican politics of many states. Its ability to impact politics, and the strategies activists use to pursue their policy goals, are shaped by the internal and external constraints placed on the Christian Right by state politics and the movement's own internal resources and ability to mobilized its constituents. This book is an attempt to think systematically about how these political processes work, and how understanding them might increase not only our understanding of the Christian Right in the United States, but also social movements, state politics, and the groups that seek influence and societal change through the state policy-making process.

# CHAPTER 2

———◦❖◦———

# THE CHRISTIAN RIGHT
# IN AMERICAN POLITICS

Christian Right activists have formed a social movement that is active around the country and at all levels. But to understand how and why the movement has concentrated on state-level politics and to understand its success—or lack thereof—we must observe the trajectory and evolution of the overall movement. Other scholars have offered rich and detailed histories of the Christian Right; I will not attempt to improve on their efforts here. My goal is to provide a brief history of the movement focusing on the mobilization, organization, and strategy of the Christian Right and its changing relationship with the Republican Party. This historical summary sets the stage for a more detailed conversation about the way the Christian Right and Republican Party interact at the state level.

The origins of the Christian Right can be traced from two distinct branches, the political activism of Evangelical Christians such as William Jennings Bryan in the late nineteenth and early twentieth centuries, and the conservative New Right movement initiated by Barry Goldwater in 1964. William Jennings Bryan, a fundamentalist populist, was a three-time presidential candidate and champion of the free silver movement.[1] His policies and rhetoric were suffused with conservative Protestant religion and he was the most famous example of the spirit of social reform that motivated many Christians of the late nineteenth and early twentieth centuries. But the rise of secularism and the theory of evolution in the early twentieth century posed a great threat to religious ways of life and views of the world. A split emerged within Protestantism between those who wanted to reconcile their faith with modernism and those who kept the fundamentals of the faith even in a changing society. More theologically conservative Protestants left the political sphere after the embarrassment of the Scopes Monkey trial in 1925.[2] They retreated to the relative safety of their own enclaves to concentrate on the purity of their religious experience. Nonfundamentalist churches continued to be involved politically, but their emphasis on the "social gospel" put them in the mainstream of politics, as opposed to the more radical alternative of the fundamentalist moralists.

In the 1950s, a new form of conservative Protestantism, Evangelicalism, rose from the ashes of the fundamentalist movement. These new "Evangelical fundamentalists" wanted to reverse the withdrawal from society under which conservative Christians had operated for a generation. These early Evangelicals, led by people like Billy Graham and Carl F. H. Henry, wanted to engage with the society around them in order to better spread the gospel and influence the larger culture. The movement formed the base of the religious conservative constituency of the Christian Right. The Evangelical movement encompasses a large portion of the American population across the socioeconomic, racial, and ethnic spectrum, but the Christian Right has proven to be a primarily white, middle-class movement. Other Evangelical-based political movements have appeared over the last fifty years. While religiously based, the civil rights movement of the 1950s and 1960s was almost entirely a phenomenon of African American churches in the South. The nearly total separation between white and non-white members of the Evangelical, Fundamentalist, and Pentecostal churches remains to this day.

Barry Goldwater and the New Right movement he inaugurated, however, provided the catalyst for the return of the values of most conservative Evangelicals to mainstream politics. While the New Right was most specifically focused on anticommunism and economic policy, conservatism of all stripes was politically acceptable once again.[3] Although he lost his bid for the presidency in 1964, Goldwater's organization consisted of newly mobilized conservatives who had moved into significant leadership positions in the Republican Party by the middle of the 1970s. Ronald Reagan's strong showing in the 1976 Republican primaries was testimony to that development.

James Guth argues that it was the national trauma of Watergate that was the early catalyst for the emergence of the Christian Right into American politics.[4] Unlike any other event, Watergate blurred the lines between private morality and public action. The consequences of Nixon's personal moral choices had a greater effect on the American public than had any president before him. This scandal served to heighten the perception of many religiously moral Americans that their beliefs had a place in American political discourse. Compounding the feeling that the end of the 1960s had somehow robbed America of its moral bearings with its focus on personal expression and opposition to traditional authorities, Nixon's duplicity signaled the need for a renewed sense of morality in the public realm.

Another proximate cause of the rise of the Christian Right was the battle over the passage and ratification of the Equal Rights Amendment (ERA). One of the oldest organizations associated with the Christian Right, Phyllis Schlafly's Eagle Forum, was formed specifically to defeat ratification of the amendment. Many conservatives, especially those of the Evangelical Christian persuasion, saw the ERA as undermining their vision of the traditional—and appropriate—family structure. Its emphasis on abortion on demand and the absolute equality of women in all circumstances ran counter to the sociomoral teachings of most Evangelical churches. Eagle Forum was founded in 1972 and is credited with exerting the grassroots influence that denied ratification of ERA a decade later by a three state margin.

Perhaps the final catalyst to spur the political involvement of religious conservatives was the election of Jimmy Carter to the White House in 1976. A publicly professing Evangelical Christian, Carter brought the notion that religion should affect politics out of the radical ends of the political spectrum into the mainstream. This further strengthened Evangelicals' feelings that they could and should make a difference in American politics. In fact, Carter's presidential campaign created one of the precipitating events for the early organization of the Christian Right. In

1976, Jerry Falwell got a phone call from Jody Powell, a special assistant to Jimmy Carter. He asked Dr. Falwell to tone down his criticism of the then-presidential candidate's interview with Playboy magazine. Falwell was shocked that the president was paying attention to what he said from his pulpit on Sunday morning. While the sermons were broadcast on a national television show, Falwell had never thought of them as political statements, but as exhortations to fellow Evangelical Christians. While the New Right had been trying to mobilize conservative Christians for several years, it seems this was the first time Falwell realized that conservative Christians could make an impact on government policy and society by simply making their voices heard.[5] From this came the advent of Moral Majority, Inc., the first wave of the Christian Right movement in America.

Another event during Carter's administration was a significant rallying point for the early pro-family movement. In an attempt to root out institutional racial discrimination in the South in 1978, the Justice Department sought to remove the tax-exempt status of many nonprofit organizations, including Christian schools.[6] Certainly many of these Christian schools in the South represented an attempt to circumvent the desegregation laws, but Christian schools all over the country fought these developments and produced a new group of grassroots, conservative Christian activists.

Many Evangelicals were not happy with Carter's performance as president. He was not sufficiently socially conservative.[7] He supported the ERA and did not strongly oppose abortion. This combined with the general frustration with his handling of national economic policy primed both Evangelicals, and more generally, Republicans, for a far more conservative candidate than they had fielded in 1976.

The late 1970s were the critical moment for the development of the Christian Right. Following the pattern of many other middle-class and identity-based social movements emerging around the world at the time,[8] a proliferation of groups expanded the reach and influence of the Christian Right in the electorate. Never monolithic, the movement spawned a plethora of organizations specifically focused on abortion, the ERA,

Christian schools, and pornography. Utilizing the nationwide network of Christian radio stations, many of these organizations were able to proclaim their messages to large numbers of conservative Evangelicals. One exception to the single-issue concentration was Jerry Falwell's Moral Majority, Inc. Calling for a return to Christian morality in all venues of public life, the Moral Majority empowered primarily fundamentalist leaders to action and mobilized thousands of church congregations. This entrance into mainstream politics, on the side of the conservative Ronald Reagan, was the movement's first appearance on the radar screen of political journalists and academics.

Tarrow demonstrates that the advent of social movements tends to happen in clusters.[9] One movement will change the political context enough that many other groups will come into being following the original's example and its tactics. Thus the Christian Right exists in the cycle of conflict started by the civil rights movement, of which the New Right was also a part. It is clear that the professionalized elements of the New Right, mobilized in 1964, played a significant role in the early preparation of the Christian Right for the achievement of its political goals.[10] They provided the mechanism, but the clearly conservative and pro-tradition message of Ronald Reagan provided the catalyst. All these forces came together in 1980 when the Christian Right was a "much-noticed presence at the 1980 Republican convention."[11] The Christian Right, mobilized by visible and ambitious leaders such as Falwell and Tim LaHaye, played an important role in starting Republican parties from scratch in strong Democratic areas, particularly in the South. The social conservatism of these new Republican organizations was central to the movement of southern whites to the Republican Party. Thus began the complex relationship between the Republican Party and the Christian Right.

This relationship continued to grow and strengthen during the Reagan administration as various candidates, backed and recruited by Christian Right Republicans, were elected to all levels of government. Evangelical Christians were also appointed to executive branch positions in the White House and the federal agencies. However, very little substantive change occurred in national policy.[12] It appeared that the Republicans under Reagan were paying lip service to conservative and religious moral issues (abortion, prayer in schools, abolition of the Department of Education), but not delivering victories of any substance.[13]

Many observers thought the Christian Right was on the wane in the late 1980s. With a conservative president in the White House who seemed to support their goals and agenda, it was difficult to argue that the movement should push for more representation in political decision making. But movement leaders realized their substantive goals were not being achieved and sought to express their policy desires in a new way.

Many of their hopes and efforts came to fruition in 1988 with the presidential candidacy of Evangelical pastor and TV personality, Pat Robertson. In Robertson, the movement had one of its own running for the highest office in the land. Large portions of the membership of Christian Right organizations believed that electing a conservative Christian of unquestionable moral credentials to the presidency would be the impetus needed to enact the reforms they desired. Robertson was not, perhaps, the most politically desirable candidate for this goal, however. He ran well at the start of the Republican primaries, winning the Iowa straw poll and coming in second to Vice President Bush in the Michigan primary. But issues of personal and policy competence and the internal theological and philosophical divisions within the Christian Right and its constituent groups (Robertson's Pentecostal and prophetic theology alienated many fundamentalists and conservative Evangelicals) plagued Robertson's campaign, especially in primary states where a motivated minority was not enough to achieve victory. While Robertson's apparent success faded away after the initial state contests, the enduring legacy of his candidacy was the number of Christian Right activists who had acceded into leadership positions in the Republican Party by the end of the general election season.[14]

In 1989, out of the remnants of his campaign organizations, Robertson founded the Christian Coalition. The Moral Majority had shut its doors in 1989. The organization had difficulty moving beyond its fundamentalist core to the larger Evangelical movement and its focus on nonsocial issues like missile defense had disillusioned some early supporters. As the more practical and local successor to the Moral Majority, the Christian Coalition embodied the notion that national politics were not fruitful for the Christian Right. Focusing on state and local elections and issues, the Christian Coalition had affiliated state organizations in nearly every state. This was the result of a conscious effort to include primarily state-level organizations that were already in existence.[15] Utilizing the support base created and nourished by the original organizations, the Coalition became truly that, a coordinator for many state-level affiliates. The nature of the issues that the Christian Coalition found to be important made its influence within the state Republican parties a major priority. With its emphasis on the practical side of politics, the organization also came to emphasize conservative economic issues at both the national and state level in addition to the religious conservative moral agenda.

The Christian Right continued to strengthen its presence in grassroots and Republican Party organizations throughout George H. W. Bush's term. The movement, in many ways, had dropped off the national political map. In the third term of Republican control of the White House, their agenda was still given lip service, if not tangible action. Most Christian Right leaders realized that they were not likely to move much further in the arena of national politics. The focus of Christian Right political action, however, had significantly shifted to the local sphere. This shift allowed the Christian Right to deflect criticism that supporters were intolerant and overbearing.[16] Moving to the smaller arenas of state politics gave the movement a connection to its own constituents that it had somewhat lacked in its earlier incarnation. It is less likely that the average voter will label their next-door neighbor, who is running for city council, an extremist than they are to a person of similar issue positions in national politics.

With the increasing power of the Christian Coalition, the focus of Christian Right political action had significantly shifted to the local sphere. Christian Right leaders, including Pat Robertson, believed that religious conservatives would have more opportunities to influence politics at local levels. They believed that their numbers would make more difference in getting the "right" people elected than seeking to wield that numeric power in a centralized way in Washington DC. Many Christian Right organization members and movement supporters began to seek positions in state and local government, particularly in local school boards and state legislatures. This trend led to the reports of school boards and other local offices being taken over by "stealth" candidates. These were movement supporters seeking votes not through the traditional avenues of party endorsement or primary campaign canvassing, but through their own internal social networks, including churches and particularly Christian radio.[17] Thus mainstream media did not appreciate their true appeal and strength until the election results were tabulated.

By the end of the 1992 Republican primaries, most Christian Right activists had accepted that George H. W. Bush, generally not conservative enough for members of the movement, would again win the nomination. While Pat Buchanan had made significant inroads to the conservative base of the Republican Party during the primaries, his rumored anti-Semitism and harsh demeanor ruined his chances to seriously challenge President Bush. Thus the Christian Right and its constituent organizations concentrated most of their national efforts on making the Republican platform as conservative as possible. By the convention, they had managed to get twenty members of their own ranks elected to the 107-member platform committee.[18] The committee drafted a platform that was far more conservative than Bush or many of the other regular Republicans would have liked. These members of the party felt compelled to stand by the platform, however, in the name of party unity in an election year. A "Pro-Family Values" TV night during the convention featured many conservative and Christian Right leaders giving speeches extolling the virtue of traditional values, families, God, and country. Many commentators have ascribed Bush's poor showing in the 1992 election to this perceived shift to the right during the convention.[19]

This election loss and the bad media coverage that followed seemed to cause some Christian Right groups to rethink their place in the public sphere. Ralph Reed, then director of the

Christian Coalition, attributed Bush's loss and the rise of the Perot phenomenon to the Republicans' lack of consistent and convinced conservatism. Pointing out the relative success of conservative and Christian Right candidates at the state and local level, Reed saw the foundations of a much more successful push for Christian Right power in the coming years.[20]

With a newly elected Democratic and liberal president, the Christian Right had a new enemy around which to mobilize conservative support. Bill Clinton gave much ammunition to religious conservatives in the first two years of his administration. His position on gays in the military, liberal abortion views, and the push for nationalized healthcare all served as significant rallying points for many members of the movement. This "crisis" poised members of the movement to seek power and influence in more significant ways. The hard campaign work by Christian Right activists and astonishing voter turnout of their rank and file supporters in the 1994 congressional elections is widely credited with producing the Republican landslide that gave the party majorities in the House and Senate. Voter mobilization by Christian Right groups in the states, in addition to general and widespread dissatisfaction with the Clinton administration's policies, led to record levels of voter turnout by religious conservatives of all theological persuasions. This unprecedented mobilization, in conjunction with an unusually high number of open seats in the House, allowed religious conservatives to be the margin of victory (estimates range from 10 to 15 percent of the voting population) in a great number of close races.[21]

The election, however, signaled a sea change in the movement and its supporters that had been in the works for several years. A focus on practical politics came to fruition. While many of the new members of Congress were actual supporters of the Christian Right, many more simply shared some, but not all of their views. The movement signed on to the conservative Republican "Contract with America," a set of policy goals that had far more to do with the economic conservatism of the mainstream Republican Party than with the Christian Right's usual agenda of social conservatism. While producing their own "Contract with the American Family" later in the 1995 session—no part of which was passed by the 104th Congress—many Christian Right activists and supporters were elected to Congress on the basis of their affiliation with economic conservatism, not social conservatism.

An ancillary effect of the 1994 successes and the rebound that followed was the increased sophistication of the activists within the states. Many came for the Robertson campaign in 1988 and the state and local elections of the early 1990s and stayed to become regular Republican Party members. As Christian Right activists "grew up" in the political arena, they moved into positions of power within state party structures.[22] This likely shifted their focus from simply election mobilization to more of a governing and policy-making role.

These changes in focus highlight the internal contradiction inherent within the Christian Right movement. A moral stance based on the Bible, which they believe to be the inerrant Word of God, is not usually amenable to the compromise situations intrinsic to modern politics. The focus on achievable goals opened up the practical part of the movement (represented by the Christian Coalition) to criticism by a more radicalized faction that believed that no compromise is appropriate. These disagreements were regularly aired in the press in the wake of the policy failures of the 104th Congress.[23] This tension led both to the creation of extremist groups such as Operation Rescue, an extremist antiabortion group that advocates violence in achieving their goals, and a move by some Evangelicals to withdraw from politics to focus on the church.[24]

The specific attention to practical politics significantly affected the relationship between the Christian Right movement and the Republican parties in the states as well. By the middle of 1994, the movement was reported to be in control of the Republican Party in eighteen states and had significant influence in thirteen more.[25] At more local levels, members of the Christian Right continued to make gains in local elections. They have also benefited from the general swing toward the Republican Party of the last twenty years. The congressional elections of 1996 and 1998, however, were not the unalloyed success of 1994. In 1996, expected readjustments were made

after the Republican landslide of 1994, causing some conservatives in tenuous positions to lose their seats as some districts
returned to their normal Democratic partisanship. President
Clinton had moderated many of his views on moral issues in
the last two years of his first term and thus provided less of a
rallying point for Christian Right mobilization. The midterm
election of 1998 continued this trend. Further, many commentators attributed the poor showing of Republicans to the party's
emphasis on President Clinton's behavior in the Monica Lewin-
sky scandal and his subsequent impeachment. This emphasis
was largely the game plan of House Speaker Newt Gingrich in
consultation with Christian Right forces. While weakening their
power in the public's perception, the Christian Right continued
to wield influence at the state level.[26]

The 2000 presidential election was a further development in
the relationship between the Christian Right and the national
Republican Party. The entire election was infused with religious
rhetoric on both sides of the partisan divide. The Christian Right
movement pressured Republican hopefuls for the 2000 election
to announce their opposition to abortion rights in the earliest
days of the campaign and at many points after that. Candidate
John McCain railed against the Christian Right and its agenda
during the primaries. Calling the Christian Right "agents of
intolerance," he denounced George W. Bush's appearance on
the Bob Jones University campus in Greenville, South Carolina,
a college with a history of anti-Catholic bias and rules against
interracial dating. His appeal, however, was mostly to Republican moderates and independents, not the standard Christian
Right supporter in the Republican Party. His candidacy failed,
in part, because rank and file Republican loyalists did not see
him as a real Republican, espousing their views. Clearly that
perception, or perhaps the Republican electorate themselves,
changed significantly by 2008.

George W. Bush, a candidate with goals more consonant with
the Christian Right moral and economic positions, was nomi-
nated by the Republican Party. While Bush publicly proclaimed
his commitment to religion and a born-again experience, the
Christian Right was conspicuously absent from the nominating

convention in 2000. In a convention emphasizing diversity and inclusion, the Christian Right was asked to tow the party line and not foment division so that the Republicans would have a better shot at the White House in November. Compliance in this area may have cost movement leaders some prestige as the closeness of the popular vote called into question the election results for several months following Election Day. Some have blamed the lack of conservative Evangelical mobilization for not providing George W. Bush with a larger margin of victory.

Many have argued that George W. Bush would have only been a one-term president had it not been for the events of September 11, 2001. While that assessment is certainly debatable, it is clear that the president's relationship with the Christian Right and its supporters was significantly improved by his response to the terrorist attacks on New York City and Washington, DC. Bush's use of biblical imagery and references in his public statements about Islamic terrorism and the wars in Afghanistan and Iraq reinforced his identity as an Evangelical believer. An administration that had started with generally inclusive language about religion and the American experience had moved significantly toward an Evangelical understanding of the world and America's place in it. His stated commitment to protect the United States and project American power in the world meshed well with the movement's focus on the Christianness of America and the importance of patriotism and love of country. The Bush administration also sought to use this support to its advantage by courting Christian Right leaders and their good opinion of the war efforts.

Bush's reelection campaign in 2004 took no chances of a repeat of 2000. The campaign started early to recruit religious conservative supporters who could drive a significant Get Out the Vote campaign, asking church members to send their church directories to the campaign for use as voter contact guides.[27] The state-level campaigns also spent significant time and money identifying Christian Right opinion leaders in their state, asking them to host a "Party for the President," where the president or one of his proxies could have direct contact with fifty to seventy-five religious conservatives using teleconferencing technology. This type of personal and targeted campaigning paid off for President Bush, resulting in his reelection by a reasonable margin.

At the state level, 2004 was an interesting year because of the presence of a new critical issue for the Christian Right. In early 2004, the Massachusetts Supreme Court ruled that not extending the ability to marry to homosexuals was a violation of the state's constitution. This, in essence, legalized gay marriage in the state. While the issue had been on the radar screen of many Christian Right activists, this development made gay marriage an important issue for the movement in 2004. In fact, much of the turnout of "values voters" in the election seems to have been driven by the issue.[28] In 2004, thirteen states held popular referenda on gay marriage; eleven in November and two earlier in the year. The issue was prominent in many state legislatures as well, heightening its importance in voters' minds. The Christian Right both responded to a perceived threat and took advantage of the opportunity to mobilize activists and voters in response to gay marriage. These efforts, combined with aggressive recruitment by the Bush campaign, energized grassroots supporters and helped the movement achieve significant voter turnout on Election Day. Observers believe these factors may have made an important difference for President Bush and Republican candidates at the margins in swing states.

Although many observers believed that the Christian Right significantly contributed to the reelection of George W. Bush and many of the movement's leaders took public credit for the victory, the years after the 2004 election did not provide the movement with the policy environment for which they had hoped. Many believed that the president would finally act on many issues such as same-sex marriage and abortion at the national level. But the primary focus of the new administration was prosecuting the wars in Iraq and Afghanistan, leaving most of its original social issue agenda to die on the vine. Only two years later, the Republicans suffered significant defeat in the 2006 midterm elections, losing both houses of Congress. Some observers suggest that many Evangelicals, the primary constituency of the Christian Right, were frustrated both with President

Bush and the perceived rise in corruption among Republican elected officials. Small but significant numbers voted for Democratic candidates in 2006, signaling a lack of coherence among conservative voters and spelling great challenges for the Christian Right movement in the future.[29]

The great shift in Evangelical voting behavior did not take place in 2008, however. While President Barack Obama is arguably the most comfortable with religious expression, experience, and language of any national Democrat in quite a while, only 29 percent of Evangelicals, most of them under thirty, voted for him. Over 70 percent of Evangelicals voted for the Republican candidate, John McCain.[30] The real issue for the Christian Right movement, however, is the advent of a political environment geared specifically toward economic and foreign policy issues. Very few of the social issues so important to movement supporters were part of the campaign conversation on either side of the presidential election. At the state level, the movement continues to work for policy change in abortion, marriage, and education, but these efforts now have to take place in a country where most of the citizens' focus is on their pocketbooks, not their morality.

The early years of the twenty-first century have proved to be very fruitful for the Christian Right in state Republican parties. Vocal and visible movement leaders have gained positions of party leadership in several states with untold numbers of rank and file activists gaining power as well. Ralph Reed, the former director of Christian Coalition who is widely credited with the political successes of the Coalition, served as the state chair of the Republican Party in Georgia from 2001 through 2003, and was a candidate for lieutenant governor in 2006. David Barton, founder and director of "Wallbuilders," served as the Republican Vice Chair in Texas from 1997 through 2006. Wallbuilders is an organization committed to restoring its vision of America's religious heritage. He was also hired by the George W. Bush campaign in 2004 to rally support for the president among Evangelical pastors and leaders. The Texas Republican Party is strongly characterized by religious conservative activism in general. Footage of the 2004 Texas Republican state convention shows delegates singing Christian praise music as part of a prayer rally at the beginning of the meeting.[31] In addition to these visible leaders are a host of grassroots activists in positions of leadership in state Republican parties around the country.

One casualty of the growth and evolution of the Christian Right movement has been the Christian Coalition. In the years after Ralph Reed resigned as Chair, the organization went through a variety of leadership and strategy changes. In 2006, amid allegations of financial mismanagement and leadership difficulties, many of the remaining state chapters revoked their membership and started unaffiliated organizations. This removed the bulk of the national organization's financial support and the future of the Christian Coalition remains unclear. It seems a contributing factor to its demise was that the organization outlasted its usefulness, given the extensive organization and success of the Christian Right at the state level and the almost universally accepted notion among movement leadership that national politics is best influenced from the state level.

The character of the George W. Bush administration and public perceptions of the president's personal Evangelical faith have had a significant impact on the Christian Right movement and its relationship with the Republican Party as well. It has energized the movement in many ways, particularly during his reelection bid in 2004, and provides legitimacy to the relationship between the movement and party. Bush's presidency is seen as vindication for the movement's efforts, even though movement activists and other conservatives were not entirely supportive of the administration's foreign or domestic policies, especially in the last two years of his administration. Perhaps most important, however, was the personal connection many religious conservatives felt with President Bush. This seems to have cemented their relationship with the Republican Party and their commitment to support party candidates. This also played out in state politics as support for Republican candidates was equated with support for President Bush in the 2004 election.

This process of equating Republican candidates with President Bush was helped along by the Evangelical subculture. The varying degrees of grassroots activity and success of Christian

Right influence in the states notwithstanding, each state movement has at its root a core of Evangelical churches and organizations that provide the majority of its constituency and the vehicles through which much information and opinion is disseminated. Evangelical churches provide fertile ground for the mobilization of activists. There is widespread agreement on moral values and appropriate behavior, with nearly all opposing abortion, sexuality outside of traditional marriage, and violence and sexuality in media. There is also widespread agreement that the society and culture of contemporary America is in many ways degenerate and detrimental to children. Further, many strains of Evangelical theology emphasize the believer's responsibility to spread the word about redemption available from these sins. The Christian Right has harnessed these beliefs into a movement. The traditions of church membership, activity, and almsgiving make the mobilization of Evangelicals even easier, as they already possess the skills of civic volunteerism so important to activism.[32] The overlapping activities and groups inherent to the Evangelical subculture make the social connections between adherents strong and continually reinforced. This holds the subculture and, further, the movement together with ties that are nonpolitical. It also builds networks of information dissemination. A person is more likely to attend to the information and opinions expressed to her by people she prays with in church and make decisions with on a missionary board than those expressed by acquaintances with whom she does not share such experiences.

As this abbreviated history of the Christian Right demonstrates, the movement has evolved into a multifaceted social movement whose focus and influence has grown steadily at the state level. Christian Right activists have grown into sophisticated political players who leverage their grassroots support into political influence in state politics and state Republican parties. Before seeking an explanation for the movement's varying influence in different states, I examine the previous research on the movement, its role in Republican parties, and more generally, how social movements and political parties interact with each other.

## PREVIOUS RESEARCH

With the increased visibility and power of the Christian Right in American politics over the past thirty years or more, scores of studies of various aspects of the movement and its followers have appeared. Much of the early work focused on generally broad overviews of the Christian Right movement, its history, beliefs, leaders, issues, and contemporary battles.[33] Many of these studies found that the Christian Right was more—and less—than what commentators in academia and the press believed. The movement seemed to be growing, with help from the older New Right movement, a group of socially conservative and politically engaged activists who were trying to use the political system to achieve their goals. While certainly amateurs in Wilson's sense of the word,[34] these activists were helping to mobilize a new voting block in state and national politics, usually on the Republican side of the aisle. While many of these studies discussed the influence and strategy of the movement, they were primarily concerned with the prospects for the movement and the changes it might bring to the American polity.

Focusing more on the sociological phenomenon of the Christian Right movement and the policy goals of its attendant organizations, other studies concentrate on the structure of the movement and its ability to succeed in modern American politics.[35] Other scholars focus broadly on particular areas of Christian Right activity such as mass mobilization,[36] influence in the U.S. Congress[37] and state legislatures,[38] local school boards,[39] or organizational development.[40] These studies give our understanding of the Christian Right depth and nuance, and demonstrate that the movement is not a short-term phenomenon, but rather a religiously motivated movement along the lines of the Temperance or civil rights movements. While more clearly assessing the phenomenon of the Christian Right at the social and political level than many of their predecessors, these analyses generally focus on the national level in their analysis of the movement's influence and impact on politics and policy. However, all point to the rising importance of the Christian Right in the states and the state Republican parties as the movement matured and developed a wider policy focus.

If these broad studies of the Christian Right are macrolevel analyses of the movement, a great deal of research exists on the opposite end of the spectrum as well. These studies, generally book chapters, focus specifically on one particular aspect or area of the movement and its relationship to politics.[41] While some volumes concentrate on a particular election year and frequently on the movement in individual states, others offer studies of the specific parts of the movements such as activists, clergy, or visible leadership. These studies allow us to understand in more depth the various pieces of the Christian Right movement. Here we find that the movement is fragmented, following a wide variety of leaders, and that the voters mobilized by the movement may look very different from the leaders and activists who seek to mobilize them. Most important, we see that the movement is not monolithic in its goals or strategies. Like every social movement, it has highs and lows of interest and impact.

Further, there is a wealth of information on the Christian Right in particular states.[42] The chapters in these books are mostly focused on those states where the movement is perceived to wield significant power. The breadth and variety of these studies attest to the wide spectrum of activities and issues the Christian Right has addressed in the last decade. They show a pattern of grassroots activity by the movement and the importance of the state's laws and the traditions of the Republican Party in each state. In many of these case studies, grassroots activism on the part of the Christian Right and the importance of effective leadership within the movement are stressed.

What will be no surprise to even a casual observer of the Christian Right is that the vast majority of all of these studies chronicle the Christian Right's political activity mainly within or in conjunction with the Republican Party. It is no secret that the movement has made significant inroads into the party at all levels. This has happened in regard to ideology, for sure, but more important changes have occurred in personnel and organization as well. Thus the analysis of the role of the Christian Right in the Republican Party infuses much of the literature in both the parties and Christian Right areas. But because the party and the movement now overlap to a significant degree, more careful scrutiny of the delicate dynamics of the relationship has sometimes been overlooked.

Early work suggested that the movement had significant influence in the national Republican Party and threatened to split it apart.[43] Further study, centered on the activists in Pat Robertson's presidential campaign, revealed that Christian Right activists were not very different from their conservative Republican colleagues.[44] This foresaw that the movement was in the party for the long term, ready to contribute time and money in order to see its goals accomplished. Later and more comprehensive work concluded that the Christian Right has been much more successful in gaining control of state Republican parties than it has been in controlling the Congressional candidate selection process in the primaries.[45]

There have been several attempts to directly measure the movement's impact on state Republican politics. In 1994, John Persinos concluded that the movement had significant influence in the Republican parties of eighteen states. Later work confirms a trend toward greater influence in the states' Republican parties over time.[46] However, only a few scholars have sought to understand the dynamics of this influence and offer explanations for its variation. Green, Guth, and Wilcox merge Persinos's data with a 1992 survey of the delegates to the Republican national convention to create an "Index of Christian Right Influence."[47] The authors find that it is the effects of movement resources that most powerfully explain the variation in influence across states, though elements of political opportunity structure are important as well. In essence, the Christian Right has more power in states with greater numbers of movement activists, where the movement has been active for enough years to link Evangelicals with the conservative activist core of the Republican Party. Further analysis of data from 2000 and 2004 finds that movement characteristics such as leadership quality and number of Evangelicals in a state matter for Christian Right influence, but just as important are characteristics of the state's political structure such as the availability of popular ballot initiatives and how closely a state monitors a party's activities.[48]

These studies are important steps in understanding why Christian Right influence among the states varies to such a degree. But in many ways these analyses present too simple a story for understanding Christian Right influence in state Republican politics. They cannot account for the variation we see in the movement and its influence and strategies among the states. It is not as if activists simply look at the number of Evangelicals in a state and divide that by the state's political context. They are making active choices about how to best pursue their goal of policy change. Resources and context are important and the strategic choices of movement activists in response to these realities are vital in understanding how the Christian Right translates grassroots support into political impact.

Understanding Christian Right activist strategy choices within each state's context helps us understand why the movement looks so different in each state. Not only does the movement's influence differ among the states, but the paths to that influence (or lack thereof) differ significantly. Therefore we can better understand both the divergent character of state movements and their differing influence by observing strategic choice in context. At a higher level, examining the strategic choices of Christian Right activists should also help us understand more clearly how social movements and political parties interact in the American context, a topic generally neglected in the study of American politics.

Unfortunately, little in the extant literature on the Christian Right in American politics lends itself to this kind of analysis of strategic choices. But looking to the larger categories of which this situation is an example, I draw from the literatures on parties and social movements for help in understanding how the Christian Right chooses its strategy and makes an impact on a state's Republican politics.

## Political Parties

A political party is notoriously hard to define. Its goals can be variously described as the winning of office for power and ambition's sake, the implementation of its policy positions, or existing as the main conduit between the elected and the governed.[49] The most comprehensive definitions take each of these into account. Parties have evolved into primarily functional entities whose purpose and goals are to serve their members and their elected officials, and to have insignificant identities of their own.[50] But parties are multifaceted creatures, existing both as organizations and as theoretical constructions for the election of candidates (voting) and the production of public policy (governance). A political party is also an aggregation of the beliefs, opinions, and needs of its constituent parts. It is one of the few institutionalized mechanisms by which citizens' voices can be communicated to the government. A party functions as the framework through which a multiplicity of goals and interests from all levels of society are debated, refined, distilled, and proclaimed.[51] In this way, a party functions as a mediator in society between the voters and those they elect. Therefore the policies and positions for which a party stands become extremely important to all those involved in the party: voters, elected officials, and party organizers.

The study of political parties at the state level is the study of fifty individual systems and 100 organizations. Much of the literature is an explication of the specifics of a particular state's laws and conventions concerning elections and the behavior of political parties.[52] Understanding that state parties function much like their national counterparts, what must we more fully understand to comprehend state-level organizations? First, state parties perform many of the "nuts and bolts" party functions, even for national offices. It is primarily their responsibility to recruit candidates for statewide offices (and to some degree for congressional seats) and to mobilize voters in ways that will coordinate their votes over various districts and levels of office. Most state parties also play a part in policy goal setting for their state, including platform drafting and coordination with state legislative caucuses. In order to accomplish these goals, state parties have formed overlapping relationships with not only local and county party organizations, but with "candidate organizations, allied groups (such as labor unions or issue groups), campaign consultants, and fund raisers."[53] Thus state parties provide a wealth of opportunities for motivated individuals or groups to seek involvement and influence within these complex relationships.

The combination of structural and cultural characteristics makes parties attractive to social movements as avenues for policy change. Since social movements' principal power and locus of activity is at the grassroots level, one of the primary political institutions with which a movement will interact is the political party. "Indeed, in the United States and Western Europe, political parties and social movements have become overlapping, mutually dependent actors in shaping politics, to the point where even long-established political parties welcome social movement support and often rely specifically on their association with social movements in order to win elections."[54] This phenomenon is well documented in the European context,[55] and though this is a rich and interesting literature, the unique nature of American parties makes identifying parallels somewhat difficult. Social movements generally must choose one of the two major parties for their political activities as America lacks the multiparty system that allows many European social movements to create their own parties. This leads to a peculiar kind of relationship among social movements and parties in the United States. Many social movements of the last century have evolved into coalition members in the Democratic Party;[56] African Americans, feminists, and gays and lesbians have all found political success as factions of the Democratic Party. The New Right and Christian Right have found their home in the Republican Party. Interestingly, however, little of the extant literature on American parties gives this phenomenon more than a passing glance.

Some scholars, however, believe that this interaction has had a profound impact on the political parties in the United States, revitalizing them ideologically and giving them a more coherent reason for existence beyond their function as service bureaus for candidates.[57] These scholars argue that current party theory is insufficient to explain the revitalization of party ideologies in the United States in the past thirty years. It is only with the advent of social movement activity in politics—based on group identities—that parties have once again become entities with vital internal debate and programmatic policy goals. Further, these changes in the parties, and the resurgence of parties in general, is a response to social movement pressure.

Goldstone takes this idea one step further and argues that social movements and political parties all over the world have become so interpenetrated that social movement activities are now difficult to distinguish from party activities.[58] No longer are social movements really insurgencies, but part of the way that individuals organize themselves in democratic polities. He goes on to note, "The influence of movements is never a simple product of the size of the movement, or of its level of activity or open support. Rather, it is the role of the movement in the multisided strategic action of state leaders, parties, countermovements, and the public at large . . . that produces the final results."[59]

The key to the relationship in the United States is the fact that political parties and social movements are drawing strength and volunteers from the same pool of people: motivated and civically engaged citizens who desire to see a change in politics. Thus the opportunity for overlapping commitments to social movements and parties is great.[60] As noted by earlier scholars,[61] and as we will see in later chapters, parties can be the beneficiary of social movement mobilization as the movement teaches individuals how to be involved in group politics and they move on to use those skills in the party context. So the interactions among social movements and political parties are very important to the dynamics of subnational politics.

These evaluations of the relationships between social movements and political parties demonstrate the need for a closer examination of the Christian Right's strategy in seeking policy change. The movement's primary constituency is in the Republican Party, and thus much of the activists' efforts center around the party. Thus, understanding the movement's roles and strategies vis-à-vis the Republican Party tells us much about the movement itself as well as its influence in Republican politics at the state level. But these theoretical approaches do not help us account for differing movement influence and strategies among the states. For assistance in examining this issue, I refer to the literature on social movements more generally.

## Social Movements

A social movement can be defined as "socially shared activities and beliefs directed toward the demand for change in some aspect of the social order."[62] It should be considered a collective action, prompted by a belief that there is something wrong with the society or its institutions in which the members reside. Social movements are formed when "individuals determine that their lot in life is not simply their own personal failure, but reflects in larger part group discrimination that has resulted in their disadvantaged status."[63]

Social movements are rarely well organized. In fact, a defining characteristic seems to be that social movement action is initially of the "ground-swell" variety. A person feels compelled to act as an individual and only after the initial deed realizes that they are part of a larger group with similar grievances and goals. Thus members or adherents do not know all of their counterparts. Most are linked through the leaders of the organizations of which they become a part as they are moved to repeated action.[64] "Social Movements are: (1) segmented, with numerous different groups or cells in continual rise and decline; (2) policephalous, having many leaders each commanding a limited following only; and (3) reticular, with multiple links between autonomous cells forming indistinctly-bounded network."[65] Further, social movements tend to encompass an aspect of personal transformation.[66] Frequently, they lead members to higher levels of political and social efficacy through shared goals and action.

One of the most widely used ways of examining social movements is through what sociologists call the political process model (PPM).[67] This model approaches social movements as embedded within the political processes they try to influence,[68] and seeks to explain a movement's behavior and influence at multiple levels of analysis. It takes seriously the necessity to understand the context in which a social movement operates (political opportunity structure), the movement's internal organization (resource mobilization), and the motivations of people who are constituents of and activists within a movement (framing processes).[69] As David S. Meyer describes it, the essential insight of the approach ". . . is that activists do not choose goals, strategies, and tactics in a vacuum. Rather, the political context, conceptualized fairly broadly, sets the grievances around which activists mobilize, advantaging some claims and disadvantaging others . . . If we want to understand the choices that activists make, we need to assess not only the resources available to groups of challengers, but also the available avenues for making claims."[70] This notion of activists' choices appears again and again because their collective actions make up the movement's behavior and strategies. Seeking to broaden the PPM theory to a larger understanding of the "cycles" of social movement activity, Tarrow demonstrates that the institutional structures in domestic politics constrain the development of social movements and contentious politics more generally.[71] He further points to the role of institutional rules in providing space for social movements to function and to the importance of the internal networks within the movement to sustain action over a long period of time. This theory and its implications for the study of the Christian Right in Republican state politics echoes the findings of political scientists who see the rules of the game as important in understanding who has power in party politics.[72]

Most important for this project and unlike most other approaches to understanding social movements, the political process model emphasizes that these constraints help explain not only the formation of social movements but also their continued maintenance and evolution.[73] In seeking an explanation for the varying influence and strategies of the Christian Right at the state level, I apply PPM to state Republican politics to account for the differing contexts in which the movement finds itself, the movement's differing reactions, and the variable levels of success the movement has experienced.

While PPM is a product primarily of sociological research into social movements, the theory has enjoyed considerable currency within political science explanations of social movement activity and impact on politics. This has been particularly true in comparative politics.[74] Within the study of religion and politics, few scholars have sought to take seriously the insights of the research on social movements across the board, and only a few[75] have even explored the implications of PPM for understanding the influence and strategy of the Christian Right. Other religion and politics scholars have pointed out that, "not surprisingly, political scientists have made their greatest contribution to social movement theory by highlighting the importance of the state and political conditions to the emergence and success of movements. Rather surprisingly, students of religiously based political mobilization have not rushed to apply the insights of this literature to their subjects."[76]

I hope to help remedy some of this lack by proposing a theory of Christian Right influence and strategy in Chapter 3 that takes the PPM as its base. Specifically, examining the context in which a movement finds itself, the internal resources available to it, and the motivations of its constituency and activists help us understand the Christian Right's influence and strategies in a theoretically coherent way.

While I am not the first political scientist to use some variant of PPM to understand the Christian Right, I believe my treatment is the most comprehensive. As mentioned earlier, Green, Guth, and Wilcox use a similar theoretical approach to determine that resources are important and Green, Rozell, and Wilcox find that the accessibility of the political process was most important for understanding the relationship between the Christian Right and Republican parties.[77] My theoretical approach applies PPM more specifically than these previous works in that it covers a specific set of contexts, resources, and threat mobilizations and demonstrates how these shape the movement's strategies and successes. Further, I examine in more depth the implications of PPM for social movement activity in American state politics.

## CONCLUSION

The Christian Right has evolved into a powerful force in state Republican politics over the last twenty-five years. Scholars have followed these developments closely, seeking to understand the movement, its influence, and how it has changed Republican politics in many states. In order to truly understand the dynamics of the movement's influence in state politics, we must move toward more comprehensive and theoretically based explanations of the Christian Right's influence and behavior. This will allow us to truly integrate our insight into the movement with our larger understanding of American politics as a whole.

## CHAPTER 3

# WORKING WITHIN, WORKING AROUND, OR GOING HOME

Minnesota is not a state where one would normally assume that there would be a strong Christian Right presence. The home of Walter Mondale and the poster child for moralistic political culture, the state has been seen as a bastion of liberalism for many years. Yet, in the early 1990s, the Republican Party in Minnesota faced significant turmoil as a candidate strongly identified with the Christian Right was endorsed by the party convention. Going on to lose the subsequent primary to a socially liberal opponent, the advent of Alan Quist and his supporters in the Republican Party caused conflict and fractures within the party for the next ten years.[1] This brief sketch brings to mind two significant questions, why was the Christian Right able to exert influence in a state like Minnesota? Why did the movement concentrate on the governor's race as opposed to other possible electoral or policy outlets? Perhaps even more interesting is the question of why the movement has so little influence in the neighboring state Wisconsin, another liberal, moralistic state. These variations in influence and strategy among the array of Christian Right movements in state-level politics lead us to seek a theory that will account for these variations and explain how they impact the influence the movement can have in state-level politics.

As noted in Chapter 2, the political process model (PPM) is used by many sociologists and political scientists to explain the behavior of social movements in politics. This is an important phrase, "in politics," because it speaks to a specific kind of social movement theory, one that takes seriously the political context in which the movement operates. PPM is generally considered to be the most sophisticated of these because it links movement resources and the motivations of activists and supporters to our theoretical understanding of the structural impact of political opportunity structure.[2] As commonly understood, PPM uses three primary components to explain the behavior and success of social movements, the political opportunity structure surrounding a movement, the movement's internal resources, and the framing processes by which a collective identity is created among supporters.[3]

In the context of the Christian Right movement in American state politics, we can observe the political opportunity structure in the "rules of the game" for movement activity. These include both the legal constraints on the party, legislation, and citizen involvement in government, but also the more informal constraints produced by politics itself: personal relationships, policy atmosphere, and public opinion. For the Christian Right, the resources it can call on in its attempts to function in its political opportunity structure are the number of grassroots constituents the movement is able to mobilize, and the quality of the leadership and organizations possessed by the movement in a state. The framing processes important to the Christian Right as it seeks to build a collective identity among its supporters are based primarily on the threat supporters perceive from the culture around them. Previous studies of the movement note how important an overall sense of threat has been to the advent of the movement and the mobilization of activists, but we will see in subsequent chapters how the perception of threat from state-level politics also has an impact on the movement's strategy and successes.

Perhaps the most important part of this study is its analysis of the principals of PPM in the context of state partisan politics. American politics is difficult to interpret outside of the context of the two-party system. There have been very few American social movements that have had similar appeal and success on both sides of the aisle. So, taking PPM as my starting point, I offer a theory of the Christian Right's interactions with the Republican parties of each state. Certainly, the importance of political opportunity structure, resources, and threat perception are obvious in the relationship among the movement and Republican parties, but given the unique nature of the American party system, a more specific set of expectations can be derived from PPM to explain Christian Right influence and strategy in state Republican politics.

To facilitate this extension of PPM into American state politics, I adopt the language of constraints. This allows me to focus more consistently on the choices that activists make and the consequences of those choices. Activists rarely separate the various constraints under which they operate into categories, but take the whole picture of political opportunity structures, internal resources, and ability to mobilize—at least as far as their knowledge takes them—in choosing the best path to pursue policy change in state politics. So, each activist makes individual choices and every movement makes collective choices about the best, most effective policies to pursue based on the array of constraints that face them.

One obvious question at this juncture is, *Why would a social movement want to use a party to achieve its goals?* As we have already noted in Chapter 2, social movements and political parties are partners with overlapping institutions and constituencies in nearly every democratic country. Movements and parties are frequently seeking the same goals using the same arguments and supporters.[4] But most particularly, social movements do not have direct access to a political system on their own. They need parties to translate their ideas into concrete policy through the political process. In multiparty systems, this frequently means that social movements found parties and are the primary players in these parties' political decisions.[5] But in the United States, where there are two long established parties that must contain a wide variety of social conflict within themselves, social movements must work to exert their influence over a party that is made up of a variety of different interests.[6] The history of the Christian Right shows its special relationship with the Republican Party, but the differing natures of the Republican parties in the fifty states makes this process of influence different in each case.

Like all social movements, Christian Right activists desire the reformulation of society based on their specific set of values and on the principles they believe to be true. Practically speaking, this means that the movement seeks to enact political change through the avenue of public policy. Thus the movement's ultimate goal is the implementation of desired policies in their state, such as bans on abortion and stem cell research and support for traditional marriage and families. The movement's strategic decisions will be based on activists' understanding of the best and most efficient way to achieve policy change. Christian Right activists follow the path of least resistance when seeking ways to change policy.

When Christian Right activists survey the political landscape in a state, their first priority is to gain influence in the state's Republican Party. They want control of or at least significant influence in the affairs of the party because it provides them with the most access to the greatest number of people. This access occurs in a context where elected and appointed Republican officials must pay attention to Christian Right activists because of their impact on party resources and priorities. Basically, the movement gets more bang for its buck by trying to gain access to the Republican Party and its organizational structure. The declining power of party organizations notwithstanding, contemporary political parties provide the network for likeminded politicians and activists to interact with each other on both a personal and professional basis. Party organizations may have focused their attention on the provision of campaign services to their candidates, but they still provide the venue through which many political compromises and policy decisions are made. Perhaps it is even due to the parties' altered status as candidate service providers that the modern party organization is attractive for Christian Right activists. The party can serve as a base to mobilize its own supporters in the interest of party, and by extension movement, goals.

The Christian Right recognized the need for and possibilities inherent in access and influence in state Republican parties early in its tenure in the American political arena. While the earliest movement activity was primarily at the national level, by the late 1980s, many Christian Right leaders were urging rank and file activists to explore the possibilities for influence at the state level, particularly in the Republican Party. These early efforts at party control tended to be heavy handed and well publicized. Factional fights in state central committees and state conventions left scorched earth between Christian Right activists and other Republicans in some states. While these defeats made later access more difficult for subsequent waves of movement activists (as we will see in subsequent chapters), they did not make the party a less attractive prize for movement activists. These setbacks only reinforced the inclination by some activists to concentrate on practical politics and success in the day to day work that truly integrates people into the party organization.

By 1994, the movement had a substantial role in eighteen state Republican parties, and by 2000, the number was forty-three.[7] These are impressive figures because they show how motivated Christian Right activists in diverse states made concerted efforts to influence and even control the tenor of Republican state politics. But the interesting story may be in those states where the Christian Right has not exhibited strong influence in state Republican parties. Why does the movement significantly influence Republican parties in some states and not in others? I argue that this influence is based on the strategic choices of the movement based on the constraints it faces in seeking to change state policy through the Republican Party.

## WORKING WITHIN, WORKING AROUND, GOING HOME

When a state-level Christian Right movement faces a Republican Party, it has three choices. The movement can work within the party, the movement can work around the party, or the movement can "go home" and not seek influence in state politics at all. Working within the party will mean movement activism on several fronts, both by individuals and by the movement as a whole. Generally speaking, when the movement chooses this route in a state, supporters are able to attain high levels in the leadership of the state's Republican Party, they are able to significantly affect the nature of party policies, and they are able to lend support to candidates for state offices who are also movement supporters.

When Christian Right activists decide to work around the Republican Party in their state, it is usually because the paths of influence in the party are closed to the movement for some reason. Working around the party usually means seeking influence in some other Republican venue, such as the state legislative caucus or through individual Republicans in state and national government. Needing to work around the party generally strengthens the role of Christian Right organizations as they become an alternative focus of power for movement activists. In some cases, the focus of movement activity goes directly and entirely to the grassroots, this is frequently the case in states with liberal ballot and referenda laws.

When a state Christian Right movement decides not to seek party influence at all, it is usually because the party and other paths to policy influence are closed to the movement for some reason. Frequently, the movement and its supporters in a state are either too few or too scattered geographically to make any kind of concerted effort at opening these power structures. While their motivations do not change, the movement's ability to enact any type of influence is stymied by their lack of resources. We may see religious conservatives in those situations move into nonpolitical avenues of societal change or focus their support on national-level groups.

When discussing the Christian Right movement in a state, I am referring to the variety of activists who are involved in those causes we would generally consider to be on the agenda of the Christian Right movement. These would nonexhaustively include the following: pro-life and stem cell issues, homeschooling, marriage definition, church regulation, and a whole host of pro-family issues. These activists are connected to each other through a variety of nonpolitical means, but are all interested in transforming society. However, it is not as if state activists have a meeting and decide which way the movement should operate. And it is certainly not the case that every activist chooses the same strategy in each state. However, I will demonstrate that in most cases, activists are choosing similar strategies in particular states. Why? Because each activist faces the same set of party and movement constraints—political opportunity structure, resources, and threat-based mobilization—and makes decisions about their ability to exert influence based on these criteria. Thus the political context in which activists and the movement find themselves is the key issue in their strategic decisions. This context helps explain not only the distribution of Christian Right influence in contemporary state politics, but also the shape and direction of the individual state-level Christian Right movements.

## Working Within

In order to understand how Christian Right activists decide to advance their cause through the Republican Party organization, we need to look at how constraints make this the most desirable choice. Social movement activists achieve the goal of influencing public policy through political parties by gaining access to a party organization itself. This is not necessarily as easy as it sounds, however. Political parties are either set up in such a way to facilitate what amounts to an insurgency within its ranks or to repel it. This translates into both constraints that define access to the party in general and constraints that determine access to the party leadership cadre. Because state-level parties are governed by the laws of the individual state, the character of these parties will vary from state to state depending on how state law has set up structures like party committees, primary elections, and party leadership selection. Further, the law may dictate how leaders are chosen, but the internal structure of the party will dictate the context in which those laws are applied.

Access to party structure describes the ease with which activists can become part of the party organization. This includes constraints like grassroots decision-making mechanisms such as the caucus or primary, the need for party volunteers and the environment in which they work, and the internal strength of the party organization. These constraints construct the ways that the party interacts and assimilates outsiders. A party that grants easier access to the party structure makes it more likely that the Christian Right movement will choose to utilize the party in its influence strategy.

Gaining access to a party structure gives social movements entry to the inner workings and decision making of the party. This allows them to "get in" to the party. Much of this access is governed by formal constraints because it is mandated by state laws and party bylaws. Thus much of this access is also fairly transparent and readily understood by movement activists looking for avenues of access. We will see in subsequent chapters that one of the hallmarks of Christian Right activists is that they have spent the time to get familiar with party and state politics to the extent that many know "the rules" better than the regular Republicans who may oppose the Christian Right's insurgency. Thus even some of the not-so-transparent avenues of influence such as congressional campaign committee staff and allied organizations have been successfully utilized by motivated Christian Right activists.

The need that almost every state-level party has for volunteers provides Christian Right activists with access to the party organization as well. Parties need volunteers for a wide variety of party functions including election cycle activities like Get Out the Vote and campaigning for party building functions like fundraising and voter list maintenance. Many volunteers go on to hold more demanding roles in other parts of the party organization, so this is a significant way for activists of all stripes to gain entry into party politics. Thus most movement activists who become active in party politics are seeking leadership positions from which to accomplish changes in policy for the party and eventually the state.

Most parties' leadership structure is built from the bottom up. These tiers of party leadership can be a blessing or a curse to Christian Right activists trying to gain access to decision making. This depends on the rules set up to fill these positions of leadership. In some states, there are numerous vacancies that can be filled by appointment. In others, there are fewer levels of leadership that can mean fewer vacancies, and in still others, the rules are set up in such a way to make it hard to fill vacancies. So, this structural dimension of the party leadership has a big impact on the movement's ability to exert influence.

Another category of constraints that impacts Christian Right activists' move up in the Republican leadership cadre is the makeup of the Republican Party's coalition in that state. In many cases, Republican coalitions are made up several identifiable groups, usually based on business interests and social issues. The key issue is that political parties are, at their core, about winning elections. Any situation or group that will tend to improve the party's ability to win the next election is likely to have an easier time influencing the party. Party elites, no matter their personal opinions or the factions to which they belong, are usually receptive to insurgencies that are likely to provide the party with a net increase in support, regardless of the quarter from which that insurgency comes. Thus the underlying dynamics of Republican electoral strength impact the Christian Right's strategy decisions in terms of the movement's ability to gain access to the party and its leadership structures.

## Working Around the Party

While impact on the Republican Party is the Christian Right's first choice, the movement sometimes must work through different avenues because the party is not open to them. If the party mechanism is not open to their influence, the movement rarely spends time or resources trying to change the structures that keep them out of party power. Instead, they find other paths of influence that, while not making their lack of party impact irrelevant, help them to achieve their policy goals through different means. Thus the movement will "work around" the party if it must.

Structural and political constraints shape these choices as well, pushing the movement toward one type of activity or another. Examples of a working around strategy include a focus on legislative activity, ballot initiative and referenda efforts, or working in the court system. These are all ways that the Christian Right can seek policy influence beyond the party. This strategy is certainly more difficult and less centralized than working within the party. It also has a significant impact on the way the movement itself operates in a state. With an effective working within strategy, the movement's organization is focused around the party. In a situation where the movement must work around the party, leaders must create alternative organizational structures like interest groups and lobbying firms to mobilize efforts. There are two major categories of constraints that lead the Christian Right movement to work around the party if they are not able to gain access to it. These are access to legislative structures and the availability of further venues for political impact.

First, and most important for Christian Right activism, is the possibility of working through the state legislature to achieve their policy goals. The Christian Right acts more like a traditional interest group in this context and is constrained by the opportunity structure inherent in legislative politics and by the laws and traditions of the individual state. As with parties, the functioning of a state's legislature is determined by state law and traditional practice and the presence and efficaciousness of other venues is determined almost entirely by state law. Therefore the political environment in which social movement activists find themselves, even beyond the Republican Party, can differ dramatically from state to state.

The leadership and institutional procedures in a state can make legislative action more attractive by offering openings for activists to influence the process and outcomes of legislative actions. One more recent legislative structural development that has the potential to increase the power of all groups interested in influencing state legislatures is the advent of term limits in many state legislatures. Term limits restrict legislators' ability to build long-term expertise in particular policy areas, a characteristic that has been the hallmark of successful state legislators of the past. This new situation requires them to rely on those people who are not limited in their ability to be involved in state politics over time, lobbyists and interest groups. Thus movement activists have the opportunity to shape public policy by building relationships with legislators who will rely on the movement for information and advice on good legislation to propose and support.

If the movement faces challenges in the state legislature or as a compliment to their efforts in the legislature, the movement may utilize other avenues of political access that allow impact to politics through less traditional means. In some states, party and election laws were written during the Progressive Era, providing more structural access to insurgent movements throughout the political process. This has allowed organized movements like the Christian Right to take advantage of the opportunities offered by this structural openness. Most important for our analysis of the strategic choices made by the Christian Right is the ability to use referenda and ballot initiatives to impact state policy.

Popular referenda or ballot initiatives are an available instrument in twenty-four states but are only used regularly in some states. These instruments provide a way for the individual citizen to speak directly to the outcome of public policy. They tend to be used in situations where popular support or opposition to an issue is perceived to contradict the opinions or actions of state legislators. The Christian Right can also utilize the courts in their attempts to change public policy. Because the courts are inherently reactive, the movement tends to use them when efforts in other arenas have failed. Beyond actual litigation, the election of judges provides another structural avenue of influence for movement activists. The election of judges allows activists to influence the judicial branch in ways impossible under systems where judges are appointed.

Working around the party forces the Christian Right to behave differently than if the movement could achieve its goals through the party. Generally speaking, when the movement can work within the party, movement organizations wither away or become parallel organizations for the training of staff and activists. This is because the party organization provides the framework necessary for concerted efforts at changing policy. However, when the movement must work around the party, they are forced to develop and maintain their own organizations to use as the backbone of lobbying and other influence efforts. The growth and sustenance of these organizations is an interesting and important part of the story when the movement is forced by political constraints to work around the party.

## Going Home

In some cases, neither the strategy of working within the party or working around it is an attractive or even a viable option for Christian Right activists. While we can observe some political action by movement activists in nearly every state, there are certainly examples of state movements that have fizzled out because of their inability to function under the contextual constraints they faced.

In some cases the barriers or opposition within those arenas is simply too great for the Christian Right to confront; they are unable to work within the party or find alternate routes to impact by working around it. The rules or the existing coalitional structure within the party may make it is so difficult for the Christian Right to operate within the party that even if activists can find a route to internal access, they are thwarted at every attempt to impact the actual operation or policy of the party. If the party has been ruled out as an avenue for Christian Right influence, the state legislature may be entirely closed to the movement as well. This can happen through a calcified leadership structure that allows no outside interference or it can happen through structure of the legislative process that make it difficult to lobby or influence members on important issues.

When both the party and legislature are closed to the movement, it tends to seek out other avenues of influence in state politics. But, these can be closed to it based on the institutional constraints that exist. As mentioned above, the existence of a judicial system that is open to influence through the election of judges gives the Christian Right an alternate avenue of access to state politics and policy. But if the judicial system in a state is based entirely on appointments, this gives the movement little ability to impact the type of people who will serve as judges. Similarly, a state with no referenda or ballot initiative provisions or those with high thresholds for such activity make it more likely that Christian Right activists will focus their efforts on individual transformation instead of political change in a state. They cannot work within the party, they cannot work around it, and so they will choose to go home when other options do not exist for them.

It seems likely that, in many cases, social movements go home for a combination of reasons. Internally weak movements should still achieve some success in open systems, but will be completely barred from closed systems. Stronger movements have the capacity and longevity to make changes even in strong systems because of their foundation of popular support. A movement goes home when it has no options, whatever the reason. In many cases, this social movement failure is cyclical. Newer or younger activists may seek influence in situations where the movement has been thwarted in the past. The struggle itself may teach activists new skills that they utilize in a later round of interaction.[8] Thus analysis of going home situations requires an attention to the changing resources of the movement and how it might mount another challenge to its society at a later time. Given these realities, it seems the situation when a social movement gives up for good is quite rare. There may be long periods of policy failure, but by its very nature a social movement will continue to seek redress of the wrongs it perceives in society.

## CHRISTIAN RIGHT MOVEMENT RESOURCES

State-level Christian Right movements themselves must have certain resources in order to be able to take advantage of the opportunities provided to them by law and party structure when seeking influence in the Republican Party. Thus, resources have an impact on a movement's choice to work within the party, work around it, or go home. This constitutes another type of constraint. A movement must be extensive enough to provide the activists necessary for party work. Basically, the movement needs a critical mass of supporters to draw on both in terms of electoral strength and grassroots work. Once a person has begun to see themselves as part of the Christian Right through mobilization and activity, they are much more likely to engage in other political activities. Thus, the main requirement for a social movement seeking to utilize the path of party influence for policy change is that there are enough people who belong to the movement to create the networks necessary to sustain movement action. In the United States, this requirement is geographical in nature. There must be enough movement supporters in a particular state for the movement to seek policy change in that state. This is true in most states in America, but in some states, supporters are too few or too widely dispersed to make an effort to impact state policy.

Previous research suggests, however, that a critical mass of supporters is necessary, but not sufficient to ensure Christian Right influence in a state's politics. The movement must have the resources to utilize such a situation, particularly good leadership. Because the Christian Right is known more for its grassroots organizing than its monetary support of conservative politics, organizational and issue leadership are the cornerstones of Christian Right movement activity. But leadership operates differently from what we might expect. The Christian Right exhibits many of the classic behaviors of a social movement including a diffuse and uncoordinated leadership structure. So, rarely is there a paramount leader in a state. More likely is a situation where there are particular leaders for particular issues or policy areas or Evangelical groupings. These leaders tend to work in conjunction with one another, though not necessarily in full cooperation. Further, the face of leadership seems to depend fairly significantly on the structure of the movement in a state. In states were the Republican Party has been strongly impacted by the movement, most leaders are involved in party politics in some way. In states where the party is closed to the movement, it tends to be easier to identify leaders of movement organizations working on specific issues. In each state, the movement's combination of constituency and leadership form the resources on which the Christian Right can draw as it makes strategic choices about its relationship with the Republican Party.

## THREAT MOBILIZATION

Another factor that can be a key issue, particularly in states with smaller Evangelical populations, is how threatened movement supporters feel by the society and politics around them. It does not seem to matter whether the threat is perceived at the state or national level, only that there is some threat perceived to the movement or its social values. Threat provides the motivation for activists to be involved in politics, and it forms the backbone of most mobilization efforts by movement leaders. In the context of intense or persistent threats, social movements tend to thrive. So too the Christian Right where most activists and supporters seem to be motivated by the perception of threat to their values.[9] But threat seems to operate pretty universally and forms the backdrop to most interactions between the Christian Right and American society at large. Without a sense of collective identity based on threat, the movement would likely have never started, let alone sustained itself for more than a generation. The perception of threat certainly varies across the states and has an impact on the strategic choices of the movement, but not to the degree of other two categories of constraints. Because it is a factor basic to the identity and purpose of the movement, threat perception is also very vulnerable to manipulation and is used by many Christian Right leaders as a potent form of mobilization.

This is not to say that the Christian Right feels more threatened than does any other societal group. In fact, scholars have shown that movement supporters do not have a higher level of social anxiety than the average person.[10] But like any social movement, the Christian Right has capitalized on conservative Evangelicals' sense that the society around them is threatening their moral values. Just as environmentalists feel that modern American consumer society is threatening their moral values. This sense of threat is used and manipulated by the movement and its leaders to mobilize supporters into activists and activists into political power.

## POLITICAL CONTEXT AND MOVEMENT RESOURCES

The case studies that follow demonstrate how these constraints operate to shape the Christian Right, its influence and strategies in three states, Indiana, Missouri, and Arizona. Indiana presents a classic case of the movement working around the party. The Republican Party in Indiana is generally closed to outside insurgency and conservative state politics makes the party less amenable to ideological arguments. The Christian Right in Indiana has focused its considerable resources on the state legislature and successfully forged relationships in that body that allow the movement significant influence in state politics and policy. Missouri presents a nearly opposite case. The Republican Party in Missouri is in many ways synonymous with the Christian Right. The movement has had little trouble in utilizing the party both ideologically and practically in order to achieve its policy goals. This has created a movement with few visible leaders, but significant impact on state politics and policy. Arizona is a mixed case. The Christian Right tries to both work within and around the Republican Party in different venues but is thwarted by significant opposition from both within and beyond the Republican Party. While the movement has had some success in influencing Republicans in the state legislature, its greatest effect seems to be in electing like-minded legislators and using the liberal ballot initiative and popular referenda powers to change state policy, thus working around the Republican Party. In each case, it is clear that movement activists are intentionally seeking the most efficient ways to use the movement's resources and that they have learned the rules of the game in their state well enough to have some success.

An intriguing outgrowth of the importance of political context is that the Christian Right will alter not only its influence strategies but also its internal organization based on the structural situation in which it finds itself. In situations where the Christian Right has gained significant access to and influence over the Republican Party, the movement will use that existing party organization to coordinate activity and achieve its goals. Therefore few social movement organizations or interest groups will form around the movement because of the superiority of the party in providing avenues for political change. However, in situations where the Republican Party is unavailable, the Christian Right is more likely to form their own indigenous organizations to serve to coordinate attempts at direct influence in disparate sectors of government. Thus, the constraints faced by the Christian Right as it seeks policy change not only affect the strategy movement activists choose, but also the shape and character of the movement through its organization and internal network.

The key issue for this study is the explanation of Christian Right movement behavior and strategic choices. Given contemporary focus on the movement's role in Republican and electoral politics, the power of this theory is in its explanation of how and why Christian Right activists are able to impact

Republican state politics in the ways that they are. The bottom line is the way political structures and movement resources shape the choices available to the movement. The Christian Right can only pursue their goal of changing state policy if the political context, consisting of both formal and informal constraints, allows the movement room to operate and seek success. Using evidence from three case studies of Indiana, Missouri, and Arizona, the next chapters test the theory and examine in greater detail the dynamics of the relationship among the Christian Right and Republican parties at the state level.

# CHAPTER 4

---✦✦✦---

# INDIANA

## WORKING AROUND A STRONG PARTY

Mitch Daniels is governor of Indiana today because religious conservatives and Christian Right activists in Indiana decided that he was a better choice than one of their own. Daniels, while certainly a conservative, does not fit the Evangelical Republican mold in Indiana. Formerly director of the Office of Management and Budget during the first George W. Bush administration, Daniels is known primarily for his economic conservative credentials. While willing to go along with social conservatives, his own opinions appear to be more moderate. This is not generally the profile of a Republican candidate that receives the support of the Christian Right when more conservative candidates exist.

His challenger in the 2004 Republican primary, Eric Miller, has been the most visible Christian Right activist in Indiana for almost twenty years. Miller has been the head of several Christian Right interest groups that lobby legislators and spend significant time and energy educating and mobilizing likeminded Religious Conservatives. Miller's influence was palpable through most of the previous ten years as he wrote legislation for sympathetic legislators and mobilized the people on his e-mail list to call their representatives in order to encourage them to vote for or against a bill. Early in the campaign he gained significant endorsements from previous Republican governors and raised over a million dollars.[1]

Why did Mitch Daniels win the Republican primary by two-thirds of the votes in a state with more self-identified

Evangelicals than almost any other state? The answer is a purely political one. Christian Right supporters believed that Daniels could win the general election and that Miller could not. They made the expedient decision that, in this case, the best was the enemy of the good. While Miller's policy stands were more in line with general religious conservative sentiment, his lack of appeal to the greater electorate endangered the movement's ability to have any policy victories. This fear was widespread in wake of sixteen years of Democratic control of the governor's mansion. Brian Vargus, an Indiana pollster and political pundit, told the Associated Press, "One of Daniels' big victories was holding together that coalition of conservative Christians and the country club corporate types."[2]

In this case, we see Indiana's Republican Party coalition working together to achieve the goal of electing a Republican governor. In a situation where a fragmented coalition could have spelled certain defeat for the party, the movement chose to be a team player for what was perceived as a greater good. This is an interesting result particularly because the Republican Party organization has been so closed to Christian Right influence in Indiana. Even though they are kept out of the party structure, movement supporters still consider themselves to be Republicans and behave in ways that demonstrate this.

The Christian Right in Indiana has had a significant impact on the politics and policies of the state. More specifically, the movement has become a clear factor in Republican politics, though not in the state party organization itself. In Indiana, the Christian Right "works around" the Republican Party organization, using its significant grassroots strength, particularly in rural areas, to influence the state legislature through electing sympathetic representatives and applying direct and indirect pressure to Republican legislators. The movement itself is fairly scattered and does not appear to feel particularly threatened by politics in what all concede is a conservative state. But the significant resources available to the Christian Right, large numbers of Evangelicals and a sophisticated cadre of political leadership, allow the movement to wield considerable influence in a state where the Republican Party has been consistently, and intentionally, closed to it.

Indiana is a conservative state and this identity is born out by the comments of many observers. It is "a conservative state as opposed to a political state," notes one. And, "Indiana is in general a pretty conservative state. Southern Indiana is closer to Georgia than it is to Michigan," remarks another. It is conservatism both fiscal and social in nature with conservatives enjoying a 20 percentage point advantage over liberals in public opinion polling. In fact, the state has a significant proportion of self-identified members of the "White Religious Right," and in the 2004 presidential election, gave President George W. Bush an 11 percent margin over John Kerry. Many Hoosiers believe that religion has a significant part to play in politics with 64 percent believing that "religious attitudes do not have enough influence on state policies" in a 2004 poll.[3]

Indiana has a relatively large population, with slightly over six million inhabitants. Over 80 percent of the population is white, making it fairly homogenous racially as well. African Americans and other minorities live primarily in the urban parts of the state, Indianapolis and the northwestern industrial cities of Gary and Hammond. And the most Evangelical areas of the state in northern and central Indiana are almost universally white. With rich farm land and a varied topographical character, the primary industries are services and manufacturing, providing a median income just slightly below the national average. The state lags behind in educational attainment with low levels of achievement in elementary and secondary education; the proportion of the population with a bachelor's degree is below 20 percent, considerably less than the national average of 24.4 percent.

While fundamentally conservative, Indiana has a long tradition of close partisan competition with politics focused primarily on the individual politician, her social ties to the community she represents, and the personal power accrued by her involvement in politics. It is a political culture where the ties of family and reciprocity dominate. One observer notes, "Family counts for a great deal. Many people argue that politics in Indiana historically has been as much a family matter as anything else." This has, in the past, created an interesting phenomenon of nearly constant Republican dominance in presidential campaigns and family dynasties of both parties in state and local politics. Because of this focus on personal relationships, politics tend to be less polarized in Indiana. Observers say that the general conservatism of the state makes many policy questions those of degree and means, with minor ideological bickering over end results. Tax issues and a rural-urban divide dominate most political questions while education quality is a perennial issue. Race and lack of access to technology (primarily Internet and telecommunications) are regionally important.

Indiana scores very high on religiosity measures of all types including daily prayer and church attendance. Over 40 percent of citizens identify themselves as Evangelical Christians, while only 25 percent identify themselves as mainline Protestant and 13 percent as Catholic.[4] Indiana has one of the largest proportions of Evangelicals in the United States. It has at least 48 Christian radio stations and several local Christian television stations that serve all the cities in the state. These media outlets provide information to Evangelicals of many denominations and help to build community and efficacy through the shared experience of listening to national speakers like Dr. James Dobson and the late D. James Kennedy. Many Christian radio programs contain some political content and an Indiana observer notes, "They [Evangelicals] are primarily engaged in the political debate through radio and television ministries, not their local churches." Correspondingly, citizens of the Indiana are overwhelmingly positive toward the Christian Right movement and its presence in state politics. However, only a small proportion of the population claims to be members of Christian Right organizations, somewhat below the national average of 17.4 percent.[5]

The Republican Party in the Indiana has historically been of the traditionally conservative bent with an independent streak. It was never strongly influenced by the progressive impulses of the early part of the twentieth century, but it also avoided many of the ideological excesses of the conservatism of the late 1940s and early 1950s. This can be traced directly to the importance of personal advancement at the expense of ideology in the politics of Indiana. Overall, the Republican Party is considered to be strong and not particularly amenable to outside influence.

Its electoral fortunes in the past decade have played a significant role in the evolution of the Christian Right in Indiana, and will be discussed in more detail below.

## THE CHRISTIAN RIGHT IN INDIANA

The Christian Right movement in Indiana is characterized primarily by the large numbers of Evangelicals on which it can draw. "I think you can conclude that the religious right is about one-third of the Republican vote . . . and that they can be activated and they have to be listened to on certain issues" comments pollster Brian Vargus.[6] While the perception of the breadth of grassroots activism varies by observer, it seems clear that many Evangelicals are involved in movement activities, either through a movement organization or on their own. One observer notes, "They're organized, but splintered. There are lots of groups, but they aren't cohesive. And they don't tend to be broad based in terms of donors." Further, particularly in the northern part of the state, movement activists are very involved in state legislative and Congressional races. The presence of large numbers of Evangelicals also tends to increase the influence of Christian Right leaders just by virtue of the possibility of mobilizing so many voters. Even when Evangelicals are not active in politics, their representatives make the credible case that the movement can command significant resources of voters and activists if the situation warrants. This seems to have produced a movement that, while having identifiable issues and leaders, is seen more as a restive potential, rather than a mobilized factor in society. This is not to say that the movement is moribund by any account, there are a number of very involved and active organizations and leaders. It is simply that the movement still has a large potential for growth if a significant threat were ever to arise.

There are several Christian Right organizations in Indiana that seek to change public policy at both the state and local levels. Most have gone through considerable evolution over the past ten years, some gaining in strength while others declining in influence. Perhaps the most visible and powerful group has been Advance America, led by 2004 Republican gubernatorial candidate Eric Miller. Founded in 1980 as Citizens Concerned for the Constitution, an organization committed to educating religious conservatives in Indiana about how government works and how to protect their religious rights from the larger society. Advance America has become known over the last twenty years as the most vocal and visible Christian Right organization in the state. Observers believe that this is mainly due to the organization's focus on the state legislature and the personal political ambitions of its founder. There are some real questions as to the organization's grassroots base, however, and some observers think that the vast majority of the organization's touted e-mail list consists of Baptist churches in northern Indiana. The organization and Eric Miller moved significantly into general conservative politics in the late 1990s and early 2000s, concentrating more explicitly on economic issues and expending less effort on social issues. Many believed that this shift was intended to position Miller to run for governor. Advance America seems to be currently in flux, with its Web site touting a new executive director, but no other staff, and Eric Miller still prominent as founder.

Several other organizations have been prominent in Christian Right politics over the past decade. Indiana Family Institute, an affiliate of Focus on the Family's Family Research Council, has a small presence on social issues in the state. As late as 2001, the organization had approximately ten staffers and was very active on a number of issues in the state legislature. But in 2006, the organization consisted only of its director and appeared to be significantly less active than it had been in past years. The Indiana chapter of the American Family Association has grown in recent years from a small presence based in Ft. Wayne to an Indianapolis office with a director and staff. Indiana American Family has concentrated primarily on more local issues with state implications, zoning, education, and more recently, the Indiana Marriage Amendment. Indiana also has a chapter of Eagle Forum, but it is unclear the extent to which the organization is active in the state, as no observers mentioned the organization in their comments.

Indiana has an active Right to Life chapter as well. Born from the fusion of two earlier pro-life groups, one concentrated in southern Indiana, one in northern Indiana, its activities are still concentrated in the rural, more conservative parts of the state outside Indianapolis. The organization has county chapters all over the state, and is active in a variety of legislative and public education functions. While pro-life groups are not usually considered to be fully part of the Christian Right, there seems to be significant overlap in constituencies that make the presence of a strong organization important to understanding the Christian Right context in Indiana.

While these Christian Right organizations lack significant staff and some currently have a lower profile than in the past, the groups are consistently active in their educational missions, especially through e-mail lists and church contacts. In this way, even a small staff can have an impact as organization supporters are encouraged to be active in politics on their own. The organizational profile for the Christian Right is different in Indiana than it is in Missouri or Arizona. Several smaller organizations are at work on various topics as opposed to no identifiable organizations as in Missouri, or a single, large organization as in Arizona. As we will see, this organizational distribution seems to be a function of the type of influence that works best in Indiana, diffuse efforts aimed at the state legislature.

One of the interesting outgrowths of this configuration of Christian Right organizations is that many activists are involved in state legislative campaigns and local politics. Observers point to the fact that while the Republican Party in general is closed to the Christian Right, there are many Christian Right supporters among the campaign and legislative staff of Christian Right legislators. It seems likely that this is a function of the traditionalist character of Indiana politics. Much more is accomplished through personal relationships than pure issue politics. These situations seem to account for the moderate level of Christian Right influence in Republican politics measured in 2000 and 2004.[7] There are parts of the Republican arena where the movement has significant impact, but not everywhere.

Interestingly, it may be the overall conservatism of the state is what prevents the movement from flexing the muscle of its Evangelical constituency more forcefully. By most accounts, regular supporters of the movement and its goals in Indiana do not feel particularly threatened by the state's policy environment. For example, the bill introduced into the state legislature to protect the display of the Ten Commandments in public buildings was sponsored by a Democratic legislator.[8] This fact points to the general consensus in most of the state concerning social issues. This is not to say that the movement and its supporters feel no threat at all, but the majority of the threat seems to concern national issues and how Indiana might be forced to follow other more liberal states in their policies. It is interesting to see how the movement organizations that exist in the state have sought to either broaden the scope of their activism to more economic and general conservative issues, or have focused almost entirely on local issues such as zoning for adult bookstores or property taxes for churches.

## THE CHRISTIAN RIGHT AND THE REPUBLICAN PARTY

The Christian Right has had a conflictual relationship with the Republican Party in Indiana. As in many other states, the movement has attempted to gain influence in the party at the state level, but has been rebuffed by both party law and internal party structure. One observer notes, "The real interesting story about the state Republican Party and the Christian Right is almost 'why hasn't the Christian Right come to dominate the Indiana Republican Party?'" Another remarks, "My impression of what happens in the state Republican Party here, is how do you get the votes of these people without having them take over the state party organization, and that's the dance that Mike [McDaniels, former Republican Party chair] has been doing for the last five years." While there is certainly Christian Right influence in the party at the local level in some areas and there has been some impact on the Republican Party platform, for the most part the movement has had to work around the party in its attempt to change policy in Indiana.

The need to put people into party offices has been a significant boon to Christian Right activists all over the country. In Indiana observers believe that Christian Right supporters, particularly in the northern part of the state, have rebuilt the local and county parties by filling the empty offices. This is born out by the number of Christian Right supporters active in Congressional and state legislative races in the north, which has led to a greater role for activists in the party organization at these local levels. Some observers further point to the overlapping identity of many of the Christian Right activists in that part of the state, many who are vocal on social issues are also in leadership in precinct and county-level Republican parties.

While access to the party itself has been successful in some cases, the party is set up in ways to make it almost impossible for Christian Right activists to become part of the leadership cadre. The processes and timing of party primaries are determined by party rules and by state laws. Thus the party leadership tends to have control over these either directly through their rules or indirectly through their influence with the state legislature. Primary elections all over the country tend to produce very low turnout. Observers point to the fact that this helps the Christian Right and other motivated minorities in their attempts to influence party politics for the same reason that caucuses help the movement. Low turnout and a motivated core of activists give the Christian Right and other social movements an edge in elections that hold little interest to the public at large. Observers believe a similar process occurs in Indiana. The lower relevance of primary elections notwithstanding, the movement can use primaries to gain access to the party depending on the circumstances surrounding the primary election. While a contested issue or prominent candidate can impact the movement's success, the structural features of the primary make the most difference in determining the Christian Right's ability to access the Republican Party through the primary.

The Indiana Republican Party is among the strongest party organizations in the country.[9] Its Democratic counterpart is not far behind it. In Indiana, the days of the patronage party—complete with corruption and clientelism—lasted into the 1980s. This was long after these types of parties had been dismantled in other states. Every state employee was "encouraged" to give 2 percent of their pay to their respective political party. Without merit-based civil service, this meant that most state employees were contributing to their parties. In fact, on the back of every application for state employment was a section for party endorsement signatures. The more important the job sought, the more signatures and the more powerful the supporters you needed to complete the application. Given that state jobs were awarded under a proportional spoils system, a Republican could apply and even receive a job under a Democratic administration, so long as the person had the endorsement of the Republicans in power. This, for many years, gave both parties a significant amount of power with the state employees and made it easier for the party to enact its policies in state government. This practice was only abolished in 1986. But the strong ties among state party leadership and government employees remains to this day. The 2 percent club significantly strengthened the party's influence in state politics.

Some say that the end of these practices, which lend themselves to corruption, really signaled a drop in power for the political parties in Indiana. That is probably true in many respects. However, the changes did not happen overnight and many laws governing the state parties were passed as the end of the 2 percent club era neared. This practice calcified the leadership of both parties in the state, keeping the same people in power over many years. So this history of internal party strength has an impact on the current fortunes of the Christian Right in Indiana politics. The movement has very little impact on the party organization itself in Indiana because the legacy of party power has created a situation that, at the higher echelons of leadership, perpetuates older party leadership that has no support for the Christian Right.

The structure of leadership choice in the Republican Party has also thwarted Christian Right activists' attempts at gaining access to leadership decision-making processes. Indiana provides what is probably the best example of this phenomenon. In 1988 the state legislature passed what is known as the "committee chair for life" law. Basically, this law gives committee chairs at every level almost unfettered control over the personnel of the party committees. It makes it very difficult for new people to be elected to committees and give the chairs full appointment rights to empty committee seats. Precinct committee people are elected during the primary election in the third year of a four year presidential cycle. These offices are frequently the only ones on the ballot at that time. Thus they are the epitome of low-information and low-interest elections. Seats frequently go unfilled and the committee chairs appoint people to fill the posts. These committee members then elect the committee chair three years later, during the next congressional off-year election. Precinct committee people must stay in office for three years before they can even attempt to affect the party leadership at higher levels. As one can imagine, this law gives precinct committee chairs significant job security. And since the higher levels of party leadership are drawn from the precinct-level committee chairs, it gives them significant power over the makeup of party leadership at higher levels of the organization.

Clearly, Indiana's organizational structure has implications for the ability of Christian Right activists to gain leadership and decision-making roles in the state's Republican Party. Many observers believe that these laws have been the deciding factor in the movement's ability to influence the Republican Party in Indiana. The lack of perceived Christian Right influence in Indiana's Republican Party is notable because of the influence the movement has in state Republican legislative affairs and the large proportion of Evangelicals in the state population. When asked about the motivation behind the "chair for life" law, one inside observer replied, "To make it harder for religious conservatives to be elected chair." It is clear then that the structure of the party works against the Christian Right's ability to have an impact on state Republican politics, and that it was intended by the party to be this way.

As we have seen, party law has created significant barriers to the movement's ability to influence the Republican Party in Indiana. But beyond that, the internal structure of the party has been problematic as well. This is primarily a result of the way the party coalition has formed. Following Indiana's identity as a traditional politics state, party factions are less about ideology and more about personal loyalty. After the 2000 election, a group of Republican leaders who were outside the state party organization mounted an attempt to take over the state party from the inside by running their own candidate for state party chair against the incumbent. Their motivation was not to make the party more or less conservative, but to remake the party into a success-ful political organization that could finally win the governor's race after sixteen years out of office. They called themselves the "Phoenix Group" because they wanted to see the party rise like a phoenix from the ashes. One observer described the effort, "Basically, this was built as an alternative party and it moved into power wholesale at the turnover. Kittle [the new party chair] raised the money to support the Phoenix Group and it had its act together when it came to power. Kittle's very strongly stated goal is to regain the governor's seat and that he doesn't even really plan to be chair after the 2004 election if they are successful." The Phoenix Group brought with them a significant ability to raise money and a much more detailed plan for creating a party that had the resources and capabilities to help Republican candidates win at all levels.

Interestingly, there were some Christian Right supporters in the Phoenix Group, but as a whole, social issues were less important to them than focusing on whatever issues would be successful with voters. Observers note that the new leadership had the same problem as the old leadership, "The challenge with social conservatives is not so much who they will vote for but whether or not they will vote." But the issues within the campaign ran in the party's favor. Indiana is a fairly conserva-tive state, so the goals of the movement were not anathema to what the Phoenix Group was trying to do, but several years of recession and a conspicuous brain drain in the state made economic issues far more important to most voters, at least in regards to the statewide offices. So, while the Phoenix Group sought to keep religious conservatives and Christian Right sup-porters happy enough to remain rank and file volunteers and voters, once they came to power in the party, economic issues dominated the scene. While the relationship between the new leadership in the Republican Party and the Christian Right was complicated by the fact that the state's most prominent Christian Right activist entered the gubernatorial primary against a candidate handpicked by Phoenix Group members, a significant split never really materialized as Mitch Daniels won both the primary and general elections in 2004 by comfortable margins.

## THE CHRISTIAN RIGHT IN THE STATE LEGISLATURE

Indiana is a state that demonstrates a classic case of a movement working around a political party. The Christian Right has had very little ability to impact the Republican Party or its decision-making structures and has therefore moved its activity almost entirely to the realm of legislative politics. The movement has had some real successes using this path, primarily through the Christian Right's ability to elect likeminded legislators and to mobilize the large number of movement supporters in the state to make their policy preferences known to the legislature. Indiana is a prime case of the movement playing to its strength in a state and achieving policy success in a state with little or no access to the Republican Party.

Government structure and the power of the government to implement policy goals vary from state to state and that variation certainly impacts the Christian Right's ability to have an impact on state politics, particularly as the movement seeks to work around the Republican Party. Indiana presents a situation with a fairly unusual set of government structures and powers. Indiana is considered a weak governor state where the legislature has primacy. While still an amateur legislature, it is considered to be more professional than Arizona's, though they are compensated at only $11,600 per year and conduct regular sessions of only 109 days. It is also considerably less amenable to outside influence than Arizona's or Missouri's. One observer notes, "The legislature tends to side with families, not experts. So you'll always see individual 'man on the street' type people testifying at committee hearings." This does not mean that there is no outside influence; interest groups and lobbyists are certainly very active in the Indiana legislature. In fact, one observer notes that the lack of campaign contribution limits in the state has given groups more impact through their ability to provide money. It is the case, however, that outside groups seem to have less influence overall than in the other two states. The Christian Right has solved this problem by working to get as many movement supporters as possible elected to the state legislature.

There are several reasons that Indiana's legislature is less amenable to outside influence. First, and perhaps most important is the character of Indiana politics. It has an individualist political culture,[10] and much of the business of government occurs unofficially, through the personal relationships of the main actors. While this has, in Indiana's past, created a situation ripe for corruption,[11] presently it effectively means that successful politicians are strongly tied into the communities that have elected them. And because of this focus on personal relationships, politics tend to be less polarized in Indiana. This situation does not necessarily harm the fortunes of the Christian Right movement in Indiana, but it does tend to dampen enthusiasm for many of the movement's more symbolic issue positions. The movement is able to work around the Republican Party through the legislature, but frequently utilizes the state's general conservatism by working with Democrats as well as Republicans.

One structural innovation in the Indiana state legislature that may affect the degree to which the Christian Right can impact the agenda is the legislative study committee. These committees meet during the legislative recess and are charged with making recommendations for legislation. They are made up of six representatives and six senators and are party-balanced. These committees focus on issues of contemporary interest to the state government, such as eminent domain or environmental regulation. Observers believe that much of the real work of the legislature is accomplished in these committees. The meetings are open to the public and their comments, but the committees form an alternate locus of authority within the legislature, where the role of the individual legislator is much more important than their partisan affiliation. Movement activists have sought to utilize these study committees. One notes, "There's been one interim study committee on the family, we were very involved. We met with them each of the three meetings, we presented testimony, we made legislative recommendations. At the second meeting we had model legislation from other states, more research."

The movement seems to have power in these committees when it has personal relationships with the members on the committee. This can be a challenge for the movement, particularly as lack of term limits have entrenched some of the movement's opponents in position of authority. This situation has reinforced the movement's commitment to electing Christian Right supporters to the state legislature. If activists are denied access to policy decisions, then there is the incentive to make sure those who are involved are sympathetic to the movement's goals.

Further impacting the ways in which the Christian Right can influence legislative politics, unlike Missouri and Arizona, Indiana does not have term limits on its state legislators. This provides a continuity of personnel in the state legislature for the movement to influence. Some would argue that this makes it more tradition-bound and calcified than other states. Suffice it to say that change happens slowly in the Indiana system. This is not necessarily a problem for the Christian Right, though, because the movement has learned how to use this situation to their advantage. Christian Right activists have long term relationships with state legislators. Many state legislators, in fact, are demonstrably members or supporters of the movement. Groups that want to accomplish change in the system are best served by building relationships with the people in power in the state. We have seen that the Christian Right has not been successful doing this within the Republican Party, so the movement has focused its attention on the state legislature. The movement has done this in two ways, first by working to elect likeminded members to the legislature, and second by traditional lobbying and legislative services functions.

Many of the most prominent and well-known Christian Right activists in Indiana are involved primarily in electoral politics in the state. The Republican Party has, over the past twenty years, suffered from a lack of resources that has translated into legislative campaigns that are more individually focused. Even the traditional role for the party in identifying voters was curtailed by lack of money to maintain voter lists. So, most state legislators have been forced to build their own electoral organizations. This situation has provided significant opportunities for Christian Right influence, particularly in the more rural areas of the state. Observers describe the movement's efforts to recruit like-minded Republican candidates and its role in mobilizing grassroots support through church and parachurch organization friendship networks. These efforts have paid off with a significant and growing number of Christian Right supporters being elected to the legislature as Republicans. Many of the current Republican leaders in the state's House of Representatives are movement supporters and even some Democrats are in tune with the movement's goals on social policy in this conservative state. Even those Republican state legislators who are not themselves supporters of the Christian Right are affected by the grassroots presence and power of the movement. One observer points out that the movement does not even need to show its power very often, "Legislators already know its [Christian Right influence] is there . . . When elected officials know they're there because of you, you don't have to remind them that often."

The Christian Right has also sought influence by traditional lobbying and information sharing methods. While there are a number of groups and individuals who spend significant time promoting Christian Right policies at the state house, probably the most important group over the last fifteen years has been Advance America, led by 2004 Republican gubernatorial candidate Eric Miller. "Miller has been a formidable force in the General Assembly on social issues, lobbying against pornography, abortion rights and virtually any proposal backed by gays and lesbians."[12] And "Miller can draw a crowd of protesters or citizen-activists like few others in state politics. He gets his followers to light up the telephone switchboard at the Statehouse."[13] He is widely acknowledged to have been the driving force behind the pro-life plank in the Republican Party platform. Miller's prominence seems to come not from the organization, but from his own personal influence and his claims to represent the majority of religious conservatives in Indiana. That assertion is certainly debatable; many commentators believe that he primarily represents his own personal views in state politics. However, Advance America claims to have a significant e-mail network and to be in contact with all the major Evangelical denominations and churches in the state. The claim to a wide constituency is certainly used to his advantage, particularly in lobbying the state legislature. One observer remarked, "Miller and the Christian Right have power because they seem to be about the only ones paying any attention. If a group can generate six 'While you were out' messages to a legislator before a vote, then they have power." Miller used this base to launch his unsuccessful bid for the Republican gubernatorial nomination in 2004.

Other groups and individuals are involved in lobbying as well. One activist described their efforts to work among a variety of movement organizations: "We'll work together, we'll discuss action items. I might call a committee chair, maybe someone else will after the hearing, let them know we're watching, let them know it's important to us, let them know it's the fourth year in a row they haven't passed a bill." So Christian Right activists are engaging in traditional forms of interest group politics, holding politicians feet to the fire. Most Christian Right leaders describe how they seek to build personal relationships with most members of the legislature and then work to influence policy from that basis. In many cases, these personal connections lead to sustained relationships where activists are not only lobbying but providing legislative services for the members, writing bills, and helping build policy coalitions. Some observers suggest that one can generally determine which Christian Right activist wrote the bill based on the member of the legislature that introduced it. Finally, many groups and individuals are involved in outside forms of lobbying, helping to coordinate rallies and protests on the grounds of the state capitol for issues such as abortion and homosexual rights. In these ways, Christian Right activists are expending energy that they are unable to use in the Republican Party to seek policy change through the mechanism of the state legislature.

The movement has not experience unalloyed success in the state legislature and movement activists are learning important lessons about how the institution works and the best way to approach it. One activist describes a situation where "the current leadership in the House will not give them hearings. And even though a lot of them members in each caucus are strong pro-life, there's another issue: if leadership won't hear your bills, things don't move. There's two things they need to do. They need a pro-life majority in each chamber and they need to have leadership that will allow that majority to works its will on bills that are important to us." Thus Christian Right activists are demonstrating the phenomenon seen all over the country. The movement can be successful when its activists learn the rules of the game and use them effectively.

Another interesting way in which the movement has been able to work around the Republican Party in Indiana is through the U.S. Congress. Many Christian Right supporters have been elected from rural Indiana districts over the past ten years. Observers believe that in many cases, the best political talents in Indiana usually end up running for national offices, not state ones. Therefore the role of members of Congress and Senators may be greater in Indiana than in other states, especially for setting the tone of politics and in framing issue importance. Senator Richard Lugar seems to fit this mold well. He is fairly conservative, and has the support of the Christian Right, but is not a part of the movement himself. But his opinions have a large impact on Republicans all over the state and his conservatism gains him the approval of all the different Republican factions in the state.

So, the Christian Right's success in electing its supporters to Congress has an impact on the movement's ability to impact policy decision making in the state legislative arena. National politicians are setting the tone and sitting members of the state legislature may harbor national ambitions of their own. This situation seems unique among the states on which I concentrate, but the situation makes sense in the context of a political culture like Indiana's, based primarily on personal relationships.

Perhaps the most telling example of how the Christian Right movement has been able to work around the Republican Party in Indiana by using the state legislature is how the movement and the Republican caucus in the Indiana House were able to impede the workings of the House in order to try to get an amendment to the Indiana constitution passed defining marriage as between one man and one woman. Indiana had had a defense of marriage act on the books since 1996, and most Democrats argue that this law provides all the protection heterosexual marriage needs in the state. Democrats believe that passing a constitutional amendment is superfluous, will unnecessary antagonize gays and their supporters, and will be a barrier for new business growth in the state because progressive companies will not want to locate there.[14] In order to amend the Indiana constitution, a draft amendment must pass both houses of the legislature in two consecutive sessions before it goes up for a legislative referendum vote in the next election cycle.

In early 2004, the state Senate, controlled by the Republicans, passed a draft constitutional amendment that banned gay marriage. The Democratically controlled House refused to let the bill out of committee and most believed it was dead in late January.[15] One observer commented, "The reason the Democrats couldn't allow a floor vote in the House was because five Democratic legislators were signed on to the Defense of Marriage Act." This problem for the Democrats signaled an opportunity for the Republicans. In early March, several days before the end of the session, the Republican minority tried to bring the bill to the floor around the objections of the Democratic leaders. They tried to do this using a "blast petition," basically equivalent to a discharge petition in the U.S. House of Representatives. After several days of wrangling with Democratic leadership, including a period when the Democratic speaker refused to acknowledge Republicans' request for the floor, Republicans walked out and effectively stalled actions on any other impending bills.[16] This effectively disrupted the end of the legislative session and was the main news story in Indiana for several days.

This story appears to be one of defeat for Christian Right members who were not able to get the marriage definition amendment passed the House. However, one observer noted in the summer of 2004, "In November, people won't remember that they shut down the legislature for the last few days, but they will remember that the Republicans were on the right side of the issue." The controversy was a big focus of the state legislative elections in the fall and Republicans returned with a majority in the 2005 session. They quickly passed the amendment in 2005 and 2006, but a narrow defeat in the 2007 session prevented the amendment from going to a popular vote. The issue was reintroduced into the state legislature in early 2009.

Thus the movement effectively used the state legislature to achieve its policy goals. The Republican Party organization wanted nothing to do with this issue and was concentrated on trying to elect a Republican governor. The movement worked around the party and effectively accomplished their goals in the state legislature, primarily through mobilizing the Christian Right supporters serving in the legislature and by lobbying Republicans to support the amendment. It is clear that even marginally socially conservative members saw the issue as politically useful, predicting the controversy would increase Republican turnout in the fall, thus increasing the chances the Republicans would elect enough members of the House to be in the majority. Clearly, their cooperation with the movement paid off.

In Indiana, we can see the ways that the existing political opportunity structure, Christian Right resources and level of threat mobilization has had a significant impact on the way the movement has pursued its policy goals and the success it has met in those endeavors. The laws and internal environment of the Republican Party have made it difficult for the movement to use the party in its quest for policy change, but the sheer numbers of Evangelicals and other conservatives in the state have allowed the movement to be successful in both electing and influencing the behavior of state lawmakers. Overall, though, perhaps because religious conservatives seem to feel little threat from state policy, the socially conservative policy passed in the state has not always obviously been a direct result of movement activities, as seen in the fight over the marriage amendment to the state constitution.

## WORKING AROUND THE
## REPUBLICAN PARTY IN INDIANA

The Christian Right in Indiana has had real success in using the state legislature to achieve its policy goals because of the state's natural inclination toward conservatism and the movement's achievements in getting their supporters elected to the legislature. The movement here represents a classic case of assessing the political options and choosing the most effective path, working around a party that was structurally and intentionally closed to them. While the Christian Right may have less impact than one might expect given the large presence of Evangelicals in the state, it is clear that the movement and its primary organizations have worked to achieve their goals in ways we would predict, through the legislature and through well-organized interest groups that serve as a focal point for information and activism in the state.

This legislative agenda has been particularly important because there is no mechanism for popular referenda or ballot initiatives in Indiana. While legislative referenda are lawful, there are significant barriers to even the state legislature placing an issue on the ballot in state. In Indiana, most Christian Right activists want to keep the courts out of much social policy decision making. This has been particularly true concerning the controversial issue of same-sex marriage. They have been largely successful at this attempt, being able to control most of the important concerns from the state legislature and not needing to use the defensive venue of the courts to protect their policy positions.

Indiana provides significant evidence for the usefulness and efficacy of my theory of state-level Christian Right influence. The Christian Right in the state has very clearly worked around the Republican Party to achieve its policy goals, using the only avenue open to the movement, the state legislature. Christian Right activists have mobilized to not only lobby the legislature and create constituent based influence, but have also become very involved with the state legislature at the campaign and local office level. In all of these situations, the movement's strategic behavior demonstrates the importance of political opportunity structure, movement resources, and threat mobilization in shaping that behavior.

Looking at political opportunity structures, the shape of party law in Indiana makes it nearly impossible for the Christian Right to penetrate the leadership structure in the party. The "chair for life" laws make it incredibly difficult for the movement, or any insurgency, to gain control of the county and district chairs so necessary for internal party influence in the state. Given that many observers claim it was enacted to protect the party from the Christian Right, this seems to be an obvious case not only of the party being closed to the movement, but where the rules of the political game have been set up to expressly exclude the movement from the process. As movement activists confront this reality, it is clear to all that an alternate method of influencing state policy is necessary.

Internal party structure provides some openings for the Christian Right movement, particularly at the grassroots and precinct level. However, combined with the effects of party law, the structure higher up in the party hierarchy is difficult for movement activists to penetrate. This is because of the traditional and non-ideological nature of politics in Indiana. As we have seen, the party is a coalition not so much of ideologically different camps, but of groups who are either more traditional or more progressive in their approach to campaigns and funding and who have loyalties to different Republican leaders. Both parts of the party are conservative, but they represent different avenues toward achieving the same goal. Thus the internal party structure, based on the way politics is carried out within the party, reinforces the barriers that face the movement in party law.

It is demonstrably the case that these characteristics of the laws that govern political parties in Indiana and the internal party structure of the Republicans in the state thwart almost any attempt by the Christian Right to gain access to and influence in the party and its leadership structures. It is also clear, however, that the internal resources of the movement, its large grassroots constituency, and scattered movement organizations, provide the Christian Right with the ability to continue to influence public policy through the realm of the state legislature. Movement activists are incredibly active in this arena, and have been very successful in electing their own to both the state legislature and the U.S. Congress. This activism focused not on the party but on alternate methods of influence has also clearly impacted the face of the movement in the state as well. While there are a number of different Christian Right organizations with largely differing constituencies, there is no single organization that serves as the locus of activity outside the party. The movement's need to be involved in a variety of different legislative functions facilitates this diffuse, yet successful strategy, even in a context where the level of threat felt by Christian Right supporters and activists is very low.

The Christian Right in Indiana is clearly active in state politics for the long term. This is not to say that individual movement activists have not tired and withdrawn from politics or that there are not cycles of activism based on social issues that come to the fore. We can see this most specifically in activists who were mobilized during the early 1980s and suffered burnout later on. One Indiana observer explained that once groups like the Moral Majority started linking nonsocial issue positions to being a supporter of the Christian Right, pastors began to wonder if the movement had the right focus. The suggestion that support of the Strategic Defense Initiative was on the same level as opposing abortion made pastors uneasy, and many began to feel their efforts were not worthwhile. This signaled a trend for pastors to go home and focus more on tending their congregations than on particular social issues. Across the board, however, the movement remains strong in Indiana and shows no signs of retreating.

All in all, Indiana provides us with an interesting look into the actual, day-to-day operations of the Christian Right as a social movement seeking to influence the society around it. In one of the most Evangelical states in the country, the movement has shaped itself to fit its political context and its available resources. Movement activists are very cognizant of the political reality in which they operate and have demonstrably spent the time to get to know the system and how to use it for their purposes. The Christian Right has concentrated its influence in the state legislature, so while the movement may have little influence in the state party, and thus in statewide races, its concentrated efforts in the legislature make it effective at pursuing its policy agenda.

# CHAPTER 5

———◦❦◦———

# MISSOURI

## "IT'S A SPIRIT THING," WORKING WITHIN THE PARTY

The Christian Right in Missouri has considerable impact on the politics and policies of the Republican Party. Like Indiana, Missouri is a conservative state where the majority of the population seems amenable to the traditional and family centered policies of the Christian Right. Unlike Indiana, the Republican Party in Missouri provides a wide variety of openings to groups like the Christian Right. The movement has capitalized on this situation, and the Republican Party is now widely considered to be controlled primarily by Christian Right forces. Thus the Christian Right in Missouri presents a classic case of the movement "working within" the Republican Party and has utilized this success in pursuing its policy goals. The party strategy has also meant a withering away of other centers of Christian Right organization, with most observers pointing to the role of Christian Right activists in the party when asked about movement influence. The presence of two large cities—with their attendant political liberalism—has created a situation where the movement feels more threatened in Missouri and has responded by being extremely active and mostly effective in seeking change through Republican politics and policies.

With a population just under six million people, Missouri is a relatively populous state and encompasses the two large urban areas of St. Louis and Kansas City. Outside the urban areas, the economy is based upon farming; agriculture and services are the two primary industries of the state. Less than 22 percent of the population holds bachelor's degrees, more than in the Indiana, but median household income is considerably lower, under $40,000. These state characteristics, primarily the importance of farming and relatively low household incomes, have a significant impact on the way politics operates in the state. The history and geography of Missouri strongly affect contemporary state politics and the relationship between the Christian Right movement and the Republican Party in the state. The divided loyalties of the state's population during the Civil War produced strongly ingrained partisanships that endure to this day. These partisanships tend to remain even in the face of ideological change, which has created a large body of conservative Democrats in the state, both voters and elected officials. Thus, while considerable party competition exists, it is within the context of overarching social and economic conservatism.

Missouri is a conservative and religious state. In fact, this description was given by almost every observer when asked to initially describe the state and its politics. With large Evangelical and Catholic populations, the state records a small proportion of "seculars," people who profess no faith in any religion with 12 percent. In exit polls for the 2004 election, 23 percent of the voting population identified themselves as members of the "White Religious Right," and in further research a large majority of the population claims to hold neutral or positive opinions of religious conservatives.[1] There are more self-identified liberals in Missouri than there are in Indiana, 20 percent of the population, and supporters of the Christian Right movement appear to have a greater sense of threat in Missouri than they do in Indiana. Another important characteristic of Missouri as a whole is a widespread acceptance of religion and religious expression, even among the nonobservant. A wide variety of vocally religious people of both parties have been elected to local and state offices and no issue has been made of their beliefs or the expression of those beliefs as elected officials. Many of the Evangelicals have conducted Bible studies and prayer meetings in their offices and encountered no opposition to the practice. The overall sense is one of comfort with religion as an integral part of life, so much so that nearly every observer cited this as a barrier to the observation of the activity of the Christian Right in the state's Republican Party.

The Republican Party in Missouri is relatively weak at the state level. There seems to be little integration with lower levels of party organization, and commentators remark that individual candidates tend to be more successful in raising money than is the state party as a whole. This fits well with the state's notion of personal politics where individual relationships are more important than partisan affiliations. According to observers, the state Republican Party organization is made up primarily of grassroots activists, without the disconnect between party workers and contributors so evident in many other state Republican parties. The state party organization appears to have a genial relationship with the Republican legislative caucuses, perhaps because the GOP has only recently become an electoral player in the statehouse, gaining control over the both houses only in 2004. This has long been a challenge in this Democratically advantaged state where party loyalties were built during the Civil War. By the leadership's own admission, the party tries to stay out of issues, except where there is a specifically political question at stake. The party as an organization appears to be fairly conservative, however, perhaps more so than many other state Republican parties. This seems to be the case both within the state central committee and the leadership within the party organization itself.

## THE CHRISTIAN RIGHT IN MISSOURI

The Christian Right movement in Missouri is based on a large and diffuse group of Evangelicals and conservative mainline Protestants and Catholics. Unlike Indiana, where support is drawn mainly from Evangelicals, the movement in Missouri draws support from a wide range of both Evangelicals and "fellow travelers" who are conservative and religious as well. Support for the movement is, as it is in many states, based in the rural and suburban sectors of the state. The profound rural-urban split in the state, however, makes the movement's influence take on a distinctly rural or "out-state" feel, and prompts significant opposition among urbanites of both parties. The

Christian Right has a significant grassroots presence in Missouri, drawing supporters and activists from churches across the state, and most strongly from the highly religious and conservative southwestern part of the state.

Missouri's large population of Catholics, and particularly conservative Catholics, supports the goals of the Christian Right in many ways. While Catholics are not usually part of the movement itself, they can provide significant grassroots and electoral support for conservative social issues. The pro-life movement, which overlaps but is not synonymous with the Christian Right, is made up primarily of Catholic activists and they are very active on life issues across the board. This has provided important support for the movement, particularly in the fight against stem cell research in the state. One observer notes of the Catholic Democrats in the legislature, "They've been able to work on life issues; they find common ground with Evangelical Christians and that would bring them more in the 'mainstream' than you would see in a state like California where there would be no olive branches."

Overall, the Christian Right in Missouri is somewhat difficult to pin down, however. There are few identifiable leaders or organizations. While most observers claim that the movement has significant power and influence in the state, when asked to name groups or leaders, most draw a blank. One observer suggested that the movement is more of a "spirit thing" where grassroots activism is based more on friendship networks than on actual mobilization by movement groups. While there are some groups, Concerned Women for America in Branson and the Missouri Family Network, for example, these are primarily either regional entities or the organization of a single person, usually a lobbyist. In terms of leadership, when observers are pressed to name names, the vast majority point to John Ashcroft and the activists he brought with him into the Republican Party when he became governor in 1985. This is quite interesting and points to the importance of the Republican Party in understanding the movement and its activities in Missouri. We will explore the relationship between the two entities in more detail below.

The Christian Right in Missouri has very successfully framed the cultural threat to religious conservatives and their values; this theme comes out much more strongly in both interviews with activists and with general observers of Missouri politics than it does in the other two states. This is unexpected, given the strong pull of general conservatism in the state. Many of the movement activists I interviewed expressed deep concerns over the state of morality in the country and about their freedom to discuss such issues in the public square. They seemed primarily mobilized by national issues, an observation echoed by other commentators in the state. This accounts for the high visibility of the issues with which the movement is involved and is a defining characteristic of Christian Right activity in the state. Most movement activists discussed abortion, education, second amendment rights, and even the United States' membership in the United Nations. While direct evidence for this is limited, it seems that the movement's framing of threat perception is driven at least in part by the rural-urban split in Missouri. The presence of two large cities, Kansas City and St. Louis, with their attendant minority populations and liberal politics, seems to threaten most movement supporters in significant ways. It is this perception of threat, and the political awareness that attends it, that has motivated religious conservatives to be such a strong force in a state whose average citizen, in many ways, holds views of society, economics, and politics indistinguishable from that of the Christian Right.

The personal and diffuse character of leadership and authority, combined with the "show-me" state sensibilities provides a unique political situation for the Christian Right in Missouri. While the state as a whole seems to lean toward the religious conservative viewpoint on most issues, the rural-urban divide in the state splits the movement's support as well. The Christian Right, however, has been highly successful in the state's Republican Party, which has traditionally been dominated by rural interests.

## THE CHRISTIAN RIGHT AND
## THE REPUBLICAN PARTY

*You don't get a sense that the religious right is out there beating the bushes because essentially they have won. And so the Republican Party has elected and recruited candidates that have fit the religious right model for the state of Missouri. So it's not as though they are actively involved, because they don't need to—they've won the day.*

This observer comment demonstrates that the Christian Right in Missouri presents a classic case of "working within" the Republican Party. Party law and internal structure and movement resources all work together to produce an open party that the movement has basically taken over with very little internal opposition. The general consensus among observers is that the party has been so conservative over time that the advent of Christian Right activists in its ranks did not significantly impact the party, at least ideologically. Further, most observers point to the party itself when asked about the core of Christian Right activity and success in Missouri. Overall, the party has offered significant access to its internal workings and leadership to the Christian Right and the movement has taken advantage of this in full force. The movement uses the party to achieve its goals in the ways we would expect; it uses its power in the party to influence policy making at all levels in the state, including the legislature, executive, bureaucracy, and grassroots mobilization.

Missouri's Republican Party presents no real barriers to the Christian Right as movement activists seek power within the party and in the larger arena of state politics. To a great degree, this is the result of the general conservativeness of the state and the party. Very few opposing voices are lifted in contrast to the movement's aims. But it is also the product of an extremely open party system, based on the state's party law that provides for numerous openings in the party leadership, and the party's internal structure that is based on primaries, lack of internal factions, and powerful public personalities. The Christian Right's power in the party is further based on the ability of the movement to take advantage of these openings.

The Republican Party—and all political parties—needs two things to win elections: money and volunteers. In most cases, the Christian Right does not provide money for parties or elections, an observation born out by Missouri commentators. As with most social movements, the Christian Right's impact comes in their mobilization and activism, not in their ability to make donations. Observers agree that the movement does provide many of the rank and file volunteers so necessary for party and candidate success in an election. Without significant numbers of unpaid workers, most election campaigns would cease to exist because vital activities would be left undone. Observers in Missouri suggest that presidential campaigns seem to be the most mobilizing and that many Christian Right activists get their start in the Republican Party through these campaigns. Working along the same lines as the activist networks mentioned above, newly active Republicans are asked to help with national campaigns and frequently become strong party supporters and activists as a result. This effect is strengthened by the diffuse nature of leadership in the party—mandated by state law—that also helps mobilized activists move up within the Republican Party ranks.

Missouri presents an interesting contrast to Indiana. It has had historically weak political parties at the state level, machine politics in St. Louis and Kansas City notwithstanding. One of the biggest barriers has been the sheer quantity of party committee jobs that need to be filled on a regular basis. This plethora of party committees is mandated by state law. The state has party committees at the state legislative, state senate, and state district court level as well as U.S. House district level.[2] Thus, there are simply more party leadership posts to fill in Missouri than in most states, and the lack of people willing to serve presents a larger problem for the state party. This is a result of historical party weakness that was not able to thwart early twentieth century reformers' efforts to dilute the power of the party by creating so many opportunities for individuals to impact the organization. Observers in Missouri believe the Christian Right has taken advantage of this situation by successfully encouraging their supporters to be more involved with Republican Party committees.

Missouri's methods of choosing precinct-level leadership, based on a varying primary system, also contributes to the openness Christian Right activists find both in grassroots activism and in moving up within the party hierarchy. Missouri uses the precinct primary system to choose its lowest level of party leadership, but has experimented with different venues for candidate nomination. Missouri used caucuses in 1992 and 1996 to choose presidential delegates, a move that provided an avenue of influence for portions of the Christian Right movement not assimilated in the Republican Party. But by all accounts, the 1996 caucuses were a disaster for the Republican Party organization and its leadership. The national party had circled the wagons around Bob Dole as the Republican candidate for president. Republican Party activists, though primarily Christian Right themselves, did not want the state to appear to be out of the mainstream of Republican opinion. However, concerted efforts by ultraconservative religious conservatives at the grassroots level, particularly in rural Missouri, delivered the caucus majorities to Pat Buchanan. The *St. Louis Post-Dispatch* pointed out, "In March 1996, the state GOP leadership and Dole suffered a dramatic embarrassment when he lost the first round of the statewide presidential caucuses to insurgent Pat Buchanan."[3] The state party organization was humiliated and got little help from the national campaign. Bill Clinton won the state by 6 percentage points. Many observers in Missouri point out that soon after the 1996 elections, the state's Republican Party changed their nomination rules and reinstated the primary as the means of choosing party candidates. Most believe this was intended to give the organization more control over the nomination outcome and was a direct result of the cooption of the caucuses by ultraconservative forces.

In many cases, primary elections hold little interest in places like Missouri and Arizona. In both states, the primaries are held late in an election season, and generally hold little interest for the average voter. The Christian Right has generally been successful in utilizing this low level of interest in their favor to nominate conservative candidates and elect Christian Right supporters to Republican precinct committee posts. In 2004, however, the Democrats in Missouri successfully moved the marriage definition ballot initiative to the primary election in order to reduce Republican turnout in the general election. The Democrats correctly believed that the initiative would encourage a significant turnout of conservative, religious voters. The Democrats wanted to vote on the ballot initiative during the primary election because they were afraid that if it were on the general election ballot, the high religious conservative turnout would mean Republican victories in the presidential election and in close state contests. The marriage definition initiative was passed during the primary election by a high margin, but the Democrats still lost significant ground in the general election. Many observers believe that Republicans capitalized on the strong turnout in the primary to identify socially conservative voters to target for further Get Out the Vote (GOTV) efforts. This is a good example of how primary elections can be significantly impacted by the presence of issues in ways that caucuses are not. And it further demonstrates how the rules of the game serve to shape the strategies religious conservatives use to achieve their policy goals.

This caucus and primary situation has set up an interesting duality in the Missouri Christian Right movement. There is a real distinction between those activists who have chosen the party as their avenue of influence and those who work in politics outside the Republican Party. While most of the state Republican leadership is demonstrably Evangelical in their religious beliefs and ascended to leadership during the governorship of John Ashcroft, there is a relevant segment of the Christian Right movement who believe that the Republican Party is not conservative enough (as evidenced in 1996 presidential caucuses). One observer notes,

> The Establishment [in the Republican Party] has some Christians in it and they've been persuaded that those of us who stand separately are bad to the party. We think we're good for the party. In fact . . . we're the best friends you've got. For two reasons: one, we're keeping those Christian conservatives who feel they have no voice in the party from leaving. Some of them are saying "why bother," or they vote for a third party or whatever.

> Plus the other part is we can help bring people into the party who felt they had no place to go.

Many of these activists, particularly in the southwest corner of the state, have started or joined chapters of the conservative group Republican Assemblies. Republican Assemblies calls itself the "Republican wing of the Republican Party." There are also numerous Christian Right activists who have chosen to work primarily on legislative issues outside of the party structure.

Within the party itself, however, it is clear that the Christian Right has significant, if not dominant, influence. The coalition of factions in Missouri's Republican Party is less obvious and far less conflictual than Arizona or Indiana's. According to many observers, the party is made up of conservatives and ultraconservatives who only disagree on the degree of their policy positions, not on the substance. While there does seem to be some division in terms of the rural versus the suburban Republicans, this is, again, a matter of emphasis, not substance. Given that many of these conservatives are in some way religious, the movement's presence within the party has caused very little if any real conflict. Christian Right supporters are found in both conservative and ultraconservative camps, so the movement tends to engage in conflicts over the means of implementation of their policy goals.

This coalition may be showing signs of cracking, however. In 2005, Republican Governor Matt Blunt supported a bill that would allow a type of stem cell research, perceived by the pro-life movement as a form of human cloning, to be practiced in the state. This measure meant millions of dollars in profits for the state's large biotechnology industry.[4] It was strongly opposed by all Christian Right activists and several discussed the likelihood of Governor Blunt losing religious conservative support if he signed the bill. One pro-life activist commented, "There was an expectation that when the Republicans were elected, that a lot of these issues would be taken care of. They are not being taken care of."[5] One observer even points out, "I think that is going to or has the potential of splitting the Republican Party in Missouri because the Governor is not favorable—even though he is a Southern Baptist—he is not favorably disposed

to this particular piece of legislation [stem cell research ban]."
While the issue was eventually put to the people in a popular
referendum in 2006, its passage only presaged more controversy in the state legislature as they debated the status of public
funding for stem cell research.

While intraparty factions have been less of an issue in Missouri than in Indiana or Arizona, political personality has played
a considerable role in paving the way for Christian Right activists
to hold significant power within the Republican Party and its
leadership structure. John Ashcroft and John Danforth, though
both formally out of office, hold sway over the opinions and
strategies of the Republican Party in Missouri. However, they
seem to exert influence in opposite directions. John Danforth
is considered to be a trailblazer, one of the first Republicans to
gain power after many years of Democratic rule in the state.
Thus his role gives him special influence in the state. Interestingly, he has used that influence in recent years to oppose the
presence of religious conservatives and Ashcroft supporters in
the party. Danforth was "among the minority in Missouri who
voted in August 2004 against the state constitutional amendment defining marriage as only between a man and a woman."[6]
The moderate, primarily urban Republicans that exist in Missouri look to Danforth as their guide, but the overwhelming
presence of Ashcroft supporters in the party organization has
limited Danforth's ability to translate his respected status into
real political influence.

John Ashcroft is now well known for his personal faith and
Christian Right policy convictions. When he was governor of
Missouri, according to all observers, his policies were not very
different from those favored by the population at large. He was a
well-liked governor and has left a lasting legacy most particularly
because he was so reviled in Washington. Missourians of most
persuasions were angered by the way Ashcroft was treated by
Democrats in the Senate during his confirmation hearings and
by the press during his tenure as Attorney General. So he wields
significant power within the party and how it views itself. Not
least, Ashcroft also brought a number of strong supporters into
the state party during his tenure as governor. This is unsurprising

since it is the general policy of most governors to put their own supporters in charge of the state party when they come to power. Ashcroft's influence is now widespread particularly because of the continued presence of his people in the party organization.

The importance of Ashcroft's supporters being in power cannot be underestimated in Missouri's Republican Party. One past chairman, Ann Wagner, was put in place by Ashcroft and is considered a pragmatic religious conservative.[7] Perhaps the single most influential party official has been John Hancock, former executive director and now a consultant in private practice acting as the political director for the party. Both Hancock and Wagner are examples of people who started out in Christian Right activism and were assimilated into the party organization. It is clear that leaders in the movement who accede to party leadership positions become assimilated into the party's organizational structure. Their goals and strategies change somewhat as they begin to view the success of the movement's agenda in terms of the success of the Republican Party. Simply being part of the party's organization seems to moderate their tactics. Assimilated activists abound within state party structures all over the country. This, perhaps, will be the greatest legacy of the Christian Right in the Republican Party: a large group of politically savvy, religiously motivated leaders who are not only ideologically socially conservative, but well versed in the ways of the party and in how to do politics.

The assimilation of Christian Right activists has an impact on the issues on which the Missouri Republican Party concentrates as well. As more Christian Right activists hold positions of power in the party, the issue positions of the party as a whole begin to look more like what the movement wants. This actually tends to make Christian Right activists less conspicuous both as party officials and in the Republican coalition as a whole. Missouri demonstrates this type of situation very well. Commentators concede that the differences between Christian Right and "regular" Republicans are almost indistinguishable. This is born out by Christian Right activists' comments as well. They do not necessarily distinguish themselves from regular Republicans; they believe they represent the mainstream of Republican opinion.

Overall, the Christian Right has a significant impact on the politics and strategy of the Republican Party in Missouri. Through the movement's influence, the Republican Party has had significant success in turning out the Christian Right and conservative base in Missouri over the last several election cycles. GOTV efforts have become a mainstay of Christian Right activism and this has great impact on the movement's relationship with the Republican Party. First and foremost, it brings more Christian Right supporters into the universe of voters the party must accommodate. This has a clear impact on the party in Missouri as their constituency becomes proportionally more conservative; candidates have had to become more conservative to win in party primaries. Observers believe this to be especially true in the suburban and exurban areas around St. Louis. Second, GOTV efforts give Christian Right activists the opportunity to identify and mobilize more potential activists.

In many cases, the GOTV efforts happen inside churches themselves. An observer notes, "In southwest Missouri, one of the biggest Baptist churches . . . Over 4000 people in that church were not registered to vote. In one week, we registered over 4000 to vote that had never voted before . . . We registered a lot of people that go to church—we did a lot of church registration drives." This gives credibility to the activists and gives them a baseline from which to gauge the suitability of new recruits. Further, GOTV efforts give activists a good taste of grassroots Republican politics. It gives them experience in doing core-level volunteer work for the party and helps new activists learn the rules of the game in their state. This occurs as the activists interact with Republican Party workers for registration information, giving them experience with the personalities and processes of state Republican politics. They also learn some of the rules of the game in terms of the breadth of conservative public opinion in their state as they interact with potential Republican voters at GOTV booths in their churches. Overall, GOTV efforts are integral to Christian Right strategies and Republican politics because they "cover all the bases." These activities give new activists a taste of political work and demonstrate the indispensability of both Christian Right activists and rank and file voters to the success of the Republican Party in a particular state.

Given that much GOTV effort takes place in churches, it is interesting to note that these and almost all other Christian Right political activities are undertaken by lay people, not by the pastors of the churches. Almost to a person, the Christian Right activists in Missouri complained that their personal pastors and those in the larger community were not involved enough in political issues. Many clergy seem to be concerned with the tax implications of political stances. Others have chosen not to address specifically political issues for theological reasons. This finding, however, does mitigate some of the popular perception that pastors are a vital link to the Christian Right movement. It is also clear that even those pastors who do discuss social or political issues from the pulpit are careful not to discuss party politics specifically. At the very most, pastors are encouraging their parishioners to vote and they may have a Republican candidate in to speak at their church, but actual party activity seems to be beyond the pale. "Supportive pastors are careful to promote issues, not candidates, from the pulpit. That said, [Owen] added, 'They've become more openly active than in previous years. They are encouraging their congregations to get active, get involved and get out the vote.'"[8] What is clear, however, is that the Christian Right movement has capitalized on the comprehensive social network that is part of conservative churches and the Evangelical subculture as a whole. Even in the absence of clergy support, Missouri's network is clearly highly integrated and functions well for the movement. Most evidence suggests that individuals are mobilized into politics most frequently by requests from their friends and acquaintances.[9] This social network provides the Christian Right with an indispensable resource as they seek access to and leadership within the Republican Party's organization. Activists have connections to each other outside of politics and have the incentive to cooperate over the long term. These characteristics give the movement the staying power and resources to conduct concerted efforts at party influence. This gives them the advantage in situations where not only numbers but perseverance is necessary.

## Influencing Legislative Politics
## through the Republican Party

Although Missouri is a classic case of Christian Right activists working within the Republican Party to achieve their policy goals, the movement has considerable power within the state legislature as well. The movement seems to use a legislative strategy not so much to work around the party, but to augment efforts already underway within the party. Some of this power is a residual effect of the movement's power within the party and among rank and file voters in the state. Many Christian Right supporters are elected to the state legislature in Missouri because many Republican candidates and the people who vote for them are themselves religious conservatives. Thus the Republican Party organization and the Republican legislative caucuses overlap to a large degree in terms of ideology and agenda. So, in this situation, the movement has achieved its purposes; by having a significant amount of impact on the Missouri's Republican Party, Christian Right activists are able to translate that access into policy making in a variety of political venues.

Another factor that improves the Christian Right's ability to impact legislative policy making is the presence of term limits in Missouri. Observers believe that movement activists were some of the earliest supporters of term limits for the state legislature. They hoped to break the power of long-serving legislative leadership that opposed many of the policy positions of the movement. One observer notes, "[Congressman Roy Blunt's] theory was that Missouri [Republicans] would never be able to take over the House and Senate unless we had term limits . . . they ran the initiative petition and got that passed and I think that it has played a significant role because you have several really key people who would still be in the senate for sure." Term limits did, in fact, remove many obstacles to Christian Right legislative influence and today, most Republican members are allied with or sympathetic to the movement. Jo Mannies, a reporter for the *St. Louis Post-Dispatch* remarks, "The Missouri Legislature always has been made up largely of abortion opponents, even when the Democrats ruled. But abortion rights forces wielded clout because they had powerful legislative allies, often the state house speakers. Term limits ended that marriage."[10] By all accounts, this change has increased the prominence of all interest groups and political organizations in the state. Most observers point to the longer lifespan of organizations and the ability of these organizations to perpetuate themselves to account for their power in the state legislature.

Political observers in Missouri note that in the state senate, legislators often refer to the approval of outside groups as evidence for the worthiness of a bill. Most observers believe that in Missouri the advent of term limits has significantly strengthened particularly the pro-life lobby in the state legislature. While it seems to give them more power, term limits can also pose a challenge to Christian Right groups. Leaders describe the amount of effort it takes to build relationships with legislators that will be replaced in just a few years with a new member who will need cultivating.

Christian Right groups in the state, primarily Concerned Women for America and Missouri Family Network, have built relationships with many legislators through their ability to provide information and by lobbying on a variety of social and moral issues. Many of the Christian Right candidates and legislators have significant networks of supporters in their districts who are not necessarily affiliated with any movement organization. So these groups concentrate on providing services for the members instead of helping to elect Christian Right candidates. Leaders have described a variety of activities that range from simply drawing a legislator's attention to a particular bill or amendment to pro-life rally events for supporters in Jefferson City and mass mailings to supporters asking them to contact their legislator on a particular issue.

The groups, however, are not the main focus of the movement in Missouri; the Republican Party is the core of the movement in the state. When asked to identify important leaders or activists in the movement, most observers draw a blank and then point to the Ashcroft group. These are the people now in charge of the state Republican Party. This demonstrates, in contrast to Indiana and Arizona, that in states like Missouri with a strong Christian Right presence in the Republican Party, the movement tends to have less active movement organizations because they are unneeded. One observer agrees, "The Evangelicals are integrated with the [Republican] party, so there's no need for a para-party organization. A lot of Republican elected officials are Evangelical Christians." But even though Missouri is characterized by a Republican Party with a significant amount of Christian Right influence, we can see that movement activists seek to influence politics in any way that they can. They leverage their party power to move policies forward in the legislative arena.

In Missouri, ballot initiatives are an available but rarely used option because the law makes it somewhat difficult to achieve the conditions required. While usually a way for the Christian Right to work around the Republican Party, in Missouri referenda are usually supported in conjunction with efforts within and through the Republican Party, making campaigns that much stronger. There were no initiatives placed on the state-wide ballot between 1958 and 1970.[11] The first time the Christian Right successfully used the initiative as a means to change state policy was in 2004, when they were able to place on the ballot an item defining marriage as between one man and one woman. This initiative passed overwhelmingly, but was the subject of a significant amount of controversy.

The Christian Right's presence in Missouri's Republican Party is so ubiquitous that most of the opposition to the movement comes from outside the party, not within it. Opposition to movement policy goals has grown up around social issues with religiously liberal activists seeking to combat the power of the Christian Right movement in life issues, both abortion and stem cell research. Missouri Religious Coalition for Reproductive Choice, state chapter for a national group, has formed the focus of opposition to the movement in the state (beyond the generalized opposition of the Democratic Party). The coalition has been involved in opposing abortion regulation and is currently supporting the push to allow stem cell research in the state. They have bought space on the billboards that line the interstates in Missouri, and are a presence at the capitol. However, given the widespread support the Christian

Right movement enjoys in Missouri, the Religious Coalition for Reproductive Choice has had little impact, but receives significant attention for its policy stances. Thus no opposition has grown up within the Republican Party to cause the Christian Right movement to seek ways to work around the party, nor has outside opposition endangered their role within the party.

The Christian Right is clearly committed to activism for the long term in Missouri. The movement has been largely successful in achieving its policy goal. Even when it fails, there is rarely any call for the movement to withdraw from politics—to go home. The Christian Right is firmly entrenched within the Republican Party system in the state and the movement uses this role strategically to accomplish or at least make visible its policy goals. Another obvious result of the movement's long-term commitment to Missouri politics is that high profile Christian Right activists tend to reappear in different organizations or campaigns, depending on the year. This demonstrates that the activists are flexible in their strategies and committed to policy change across the board, not simply to an individual issue. For better or worse, the Christian Right is a committed player in Missouri Republican politics.

## WORKING WITHIN THE REPUBLICAN PARTY IN MISSOURI

Missouri provides particularly good evidence for my theory of state Christian Right influence. The movement in Missouri works almost entirely through the Republican Party and has had significant success in using this strategy to influence state politics. There are large numbers of Christian Right supporters who are active in the Republican Party at all levels. Most commentators not only note this situation, but point to the party when asked about Christian Right activities overall. The movement and the party apparently seem synonymous to most observers. This significant overlap has had some interesting effects for the Christian Right movement; there are very few movement organizations in the state because the locus of activity is the party. Further, commentators believe that the general conservatism of Republicans in Missouri masks the true impact of the Christian Right on the Republican Party. These observers say the movement has significant power, but because many Republicans share the Christian Right's issue positions, the changes in the party over the last twenty years have been less obvious.

The political opportunity structure in the state is very amenable to the activities and influence of the Christian Right. The structure of party law in Missouri makes it very easy for movements like the Christian Right to gain access to the party. The large numbers of party committees mandated by state law create the need for large numbers of volunteers to serve on these committees, a situation of which, by all accounts, the Christian Right has taken advantage. This further affects the internal structure of the party. Broadly based access to the party itself weakens the party's ability to hold off insurgencies. In the case of the Christian Right, however, there seemed to be little opposition within the party to the movement's advent. John Ashcroft's election and the personnel he brought to the party seem to have been a watershed for the Christian Right in the Republican Party, but it did not represent a significant ideological change. Thus, we can see that in Missouri, both party laws and internal party structure were aligned in ways that made the ascent of the Christian Right not only possible, but generally welcomed. Overall, the strength of the movement and its wide grassroots support allow it to take advantage of the political structure under which the movement operates.

The Christian Right in Missouri offers a glimpse of a movement very different from that in Indiana. It demonstrates to us the wide variety of social and political ingredients that can mold a successful movement. Clearly, there is no single pattern of success for the Christian Right. But the political opportunity structure, movement resources, and level of threat mobilization in the Christian Right also demonstrably affect the movement's organization and its ability to achieve its policy goals. Movement activists are no less savvy or committed than in Indiana, but their scope of action is quite different. We must look to the power centers in the Republican Party to see the real faces of the Christian Right in Missouri.

# CHAPTER 6

—◆◆◆—

# ARIZONA

## COVERING THE BASES IN A WEAK PARTY STATE

*In Arizona, the political system is really a free-for-all. You're a
native after about a year and a half. So there isn't the structure
of other states where you have to work through the ranks in order to
become senior and important enough to run for office.*

—Anonymous

The Christian Right in Arizona has had limited success in
impacting Republican politics and public policy. The movement is very active, however, and primarily utilizes a working
around strategy in its relationship with the Republican Party.
The resources of a significant Evangelical population along with
strong and focused leadership have given the Christian Right the
ability to take advantage of the limited opportunities Arizona's
political context can afford. The Christian Right faces a weak
Republican Party rent by conflict and a state political climate that
is generally unfriendly to religious conservative values. While the
movement has had some success in state legislative efforts, the
clearest evidence of the movement's activity—though not necessarily successful—has been in the realm of ballot initiatives and
popular referenda. The Christian Right in Arizona is a prime
example of the ways in which state political context shapes the
movement's ability to transform society.

Arizona is, in many ways, the last bastion of the Old West
in the United States. Numbering a little over five million,

Arizona's population is concentrated in two main urban areas. The Phoenix/Maricopa county area contains 60 percent of the state's population and the Tucson/Pima county area contains another 16 percent. Arizona, its people, and in many cases its politics, are determined by geography. Less than 20 percent of the land in Arizona is privately owned.[1] The rest is owned by the state, the U.S. government, or by Native American tribes. Phoenix is now a sprawling city of over three million people with a greater land area than Los Angeles. Most of Arizona is desert or other marginal grassland, so the need for water and the rights to that water are perennial questions in state politics. While agriculture and ranching were historically important to Arizona's economy, the state has now moved to a service-based economy, focused around the population centers. Arizona is also a very transient state that has experienced explosive growth over the last twenty-five years. Observers say that for every five people who relocate to Arizona, four leave. This has caused what observers call a weak social structure with very few of the established people in business and politics that form the upper levels of social and political leadership in most states. The state's median household income, at just over $42,500 per year, is just below the national average, as is the number of people holding bachelor's degrees, 23.5 percent.

Arizona takes its identity as a Western state very seriously. As the last of the forty-eight continental states to join the Union, Arizonans relish the idea that the state is still part of the American frontier. In many ways, the state remained a frontier, sparsely populated and remote, until the advent of affordable home air-conditioning in the 1960s. Arizona is also a bastion of the anti-federal government sentiment that is a significant factor in Mountain West states. The "Wild West" ethic, combined with the federal government's control of the vast majority of the land and water, a significant Mormon population (including several breakaway polygamous communities in northern Arizona), and the politics of Barry Goldwater all combine to provide the state with a contemporary self-concept that is very individualistic and self-reliant. This has lead to the strong strain of libertarianism that can be observed in the Republican Party and other parts of Arizona politics. This libertarian bent, plus a significant urban population, makes Arizonans less conservative overall than the citizens of Indiana or Missouri. Observers also believe that more and more of the state's in-migration is coming from California, bringing more moderate Republicans to the state. Antigovernment sentiment aside, the state is more likely to support conservative financial policy with very liberal social policy—a situation that makes the policy goals of the Christian Right difficult to achieve.

Arizona is quite diverse religiously, though it ranks fairly low among states in terms of religiosity and religious practice. Evangelicals make up the largest single group with approximately 25 percent of the population, but Catholics are a close second with 20 percent. The strong presence of Latinos in Arizona, both immigrant and native born, give the Catholic Church much of its appeal. However, less than half of these Catholics consider themselves to be observant and attend Mass at least once a week. Mainline Protestants make up about 15 percent of the population, seculars 11 percent, and Mormons, approximately 8 percent. Arizonans are also more likely to have an unfavorable opinion of the Christian Right than the national average; 41 percent hold this opinion, compared to 37 percent of the nation as a whole.[2] The perception of most observers is that Arizonans are largely indifferent to religion and oppose the type of policies that most religious conservatives support. This makes for a difficult policy environment for Christian Right activists.

Arizona's Republican Party is considered weak by scholars and state observers alike. There seems to be significant disconnect between the leadership and rank and file members on issues and strategy. This is exacerbated by Arizona's election laws that provide candidates with the ability to run outside the party purview with public funding. Observers and pundits tell stories of significant internal conflict and an inability to articulate comprehensive party goals.[3] Political parties in general are weak in Arizona, however. As is the case with most government functions in the state, citizens want a system where institutions have as little power as possible to control their daily lives. So a weak and conflicted Republican Party is what we would expect from such a political culture.

## THE CHRISTIAN RIGHT IN ARIZONA

In many ways, the Christian Right faces an uphill battle in Arizona. While able to draw on sizable grassroots support, the political culture and social structure of the state make it somewhat difficult to capitalize on this resource. The movement is characterized primarily by the relatively large Evangelical population in the state. There are also active populations of conservative Catholics and Mormons in the state, but observers believe that coordination among the groups has been difficult because of the theological differences among them. Christian Right activity is concentrated in Phoenix and in the vast suburbs around the state capital. As in Indiana and Missouri, activists are connected in a network of issues and campaigns, but uniquely in Arizona, most of the movement activity and strategy seems to be coordinated by the Center for Arizona Policy.

Mirroring the situation in other states, Christian Right organizations tend to be the locus of activity for the movement in Arizona. There are a wide variety of groups in the state representing a multitude of single issues and all three of the major religious traditions concerned with pro-family legislation, Evangelicals, Mormons, and Catholics. Because theological and cultural issues tend to keep these groups apart, a single organization has emerged that serves as a clearinghouse for information and strategy, the Evangelical Center for Arizona Policy. An affiliate of the national Family Research Council, it is clear from both participants and observers that the Center for Arizona Policy is the most vocal and visible Christian Right group within state politics. Most observers point to the group's importance when asked about prominent Christian Right voices in the state and the state legislature. The group is organized both to lobby the legislature and to educate and mobilize grassroots activism and its Web site claims that it is the largest family policy council in the United States. According to observers, Center staffers pay close attention to the legislative agendas and floor activities of both parties, and when the legislature is out of session, staffers spend their time identifying important policy goals and possible upcoming conflicts. The Center for Arizona Policy drafts legislation and seeks to form relationships with like-minded legislators. They claim to be active on a wide variety of issues including abortion, education, parenting, religious freedom, and marriage.

The most prominent leader in the state's movement is the former director of the Center for Arizona Politics, Len Munsil. He ran for governor in 2006, winning the Republican primary, but losing the general election to the incumbent Democratic governor, Janet Napolitano. Munsil had been the director of the Center since its reorganization in 1995 and had built up a reputation as the most visible spokesperson for the Christian Right in the state. After losing the election, he went on to form the political action committee "Principled Reaganesque Outcomes" in 2007 to support conservative politics in Arizona. His continued influence on the state and the movement is unclear, but the Center for Arizona Policy continues as the primary Christian Right organization and policy clearinghouse in the state.

One of the unique characteristics of the Christian Right in Arizona is the presence of a significant Mormon population in the state. Scholars disagree on whether to include Mormons in studies of the Christian Right for many of the same reasons that they a pose a problem for the Evangelical-based movement in Arizona. While Mormons' policy goals, overall conservatism, and commitment to Republican politics mirror and even exceed that of Evangelicals, they organize and operate very differently. Because their theological differences separate them from the mainstream of Evangelicals in the United States, it is unclear the extent to which they should be considered part of the Christian Right movement. Most observers believe religious conservatives and Latter-Day Saints (LDS) to be "co-belligerents" on many issues and Christian Right activists in Arizona make a point in emphasizing their willingness to work with Mormons at all levels of policy influence. But Mormons are more likely to join political organizations run by their own coreligionists. Part of the problem lies in the distinct theological differences that separate the groups and make it difficult for

Mormons to ascend to leadership positions in Evangelical organizations. Less charitable observers believe that LDS leaders are more assertive in telling their parishioners, both rank and file and elected officials, what are appropriate policy positions and how to vote. As a historically persecuted minority, Mormons tend to isolate themselves geographically as well. The influence of the LDS Church and affiliated social and political organizations is somewhat of an enigma for Christian Right activists. While the two groups certainly share goals, barriers exist that prevent full cooperation. So while Christian Right organizations can generally expect support for their policy initiatives, lack of coordination thwarts success.

Overall, the Christian Right in Arizona feels very threatened by the state political and social context in which they operate. In a state with high transience, a relatively large gay and lesbian population, a Republican Party with a strong libertarian streak, and high levels of secularism and opposition to Christian Right issues, the movement perceives itself to be directly threatened on most fronts. This seems to create a situation where activists are very involved and committed, but have little to show for their efforts in terms of policy. Arizona presents a clear case where the Christian Right's fortunes are strongly regulated by the larger state context and political opportunity structure. It is only the movement's high degree of organization and motivation, capitalizing on the resources at its disposal that helps to partially overcome a very difficult political and structural situation.

## THE CHRISTIAN RIGHT AND THE REPUBLICAN PARTY

Arizona presents an interesting situation where the Christian Right works both within and around the state Republican Party. There are some avenues of access to the party, particularly at the grassroots level, but the internal structure of the party makes it difficult for the movement to utilize the party to change public policy. The movement also seeks to change public policy through the avenues of the legislature and popular referenda. In no case is the Christian Right entirely successful, but the combination of strategies helps the movement to achieve what success it can.

Arizona's party system is among the weakest in the United States.[4] It was formed during the Progressive Era and designed to allow as much citizen access as possible. The same could be said of the governmental system as a whole. This situation makes it very difficult for the Christian Right, or any insurgent group, to fully utilize the Republican Party to affect public policy. Many observers believe that Arizona is several years behind the rest of the country in the battles being fought within the Republican Party and in the relationship among the Christian Right and more moderate groups within the Republican Party. One observer notes, "Evangelical politics is an old enough movement now that they are split on style, between being right and winning. Arizona is probably six to eight years behind the rest of the country on the conservative-moderate split in the party. They are fighting wars that happened a decade ago in other states." In Arizona, it is the lack of social structure that has defined how the party operates and the ways in which the Christian Right has sought influence in the party. In most states, there are "elder statesmen" within the party who are able, if not to control the party organization, then to serve as touchstones for the parameters of acceptable behavior. Arizona has no such "grand old men," and it is the state's social character and migration patterns that have contributed to this absence, as has recent Republican history. Says one observer, "Arizona has no social structure. This is a core problem in politics in general and in the Republican Party in particular. If you go off the deep end, there aren't five old guard people to come have lunch with you and tell you to knock it off. That exists in other states, even with weak parties. So there are no consequences for bad behavior."

Perhaps most difficult for Arizona parties has been the advent of the "Clean Elections" law, passed by ballot initiative in 1998. This publicly funded campaign finance system requires participating candidates to accept only $5 donations from people in their district and refuse all other campaign contributions. Their campaigns are paid for with state money and the candidates must comply with strict expenditure limits. The idea behind the plan was to increase citizen participation in government and help elect legislators who do not owe their seats to any type of campaign contributor. The unintended consequence of this has been a further weakening of Arizona's political parties. One observer notes that if the party cannot endorse or support candidates financially, it has no real reason to exist. As of the 2004 election cycle, ten of the eleven statewide office holders, thirty-five of the sixty Arizona House members and seven of the thirty Senators participated in the Clean Elections financing system.[5]

The advent of Clean Elections in Arizona has removed the locus of power in campaigns away from the political parties. These changes in law that made parties less relevant, combined with the transience of the population, particularly in Phoenix, created a situation where few of the lower-level Republican Party offices have been filled. This has allowed Christian Right supporters, in particular pro-life activists, an avenue for access into the party. While this has translated into movement strength in parts of the Republican Party, the organization is not uniformly impacted. All parties need volunteers in order to operate, and the Christian Right can offer bodies as a resource to the party. In some areas, the movement has been successful in leveraging this into party representation at the grassroots level, but because neighborhoods—particularly in Phoenix—tend to be fairly homogenous, this strategy has only worked in those areas where there are pro-life Republicans.

Arizona uses a primary system to select its precinct committees, but these elections are the epitome of low-interest and low-profile elections. Arizona's primaries are held in September of election years and rarely turn out more than 15 percent of the voting public. While certainly a potential avenue for Christian Right success, again, this has only been successful in limited geographic areas, at least in terms of party politics. Legislative politics seems to be a slightly different story as we will see below. Beyond the efforts of the Christian Right to mobilize supporters to turn out to vote for sympathetic precinct committee people is the effort to recruit these precinct committee people in the first place. In precincts all over the country, there are enormous numbers of empty seats because of lack of interest by the local rank and file Republicans. Observers believe that the Christian Right has recognized the situation and sought to remedy it both by standing candidates for precinct roles as well as getting supporters appointed to seats unfilled during elections. Christian Right activists and leaders of movement organizations in several states have commented that they actively encourage their supporters to run for Republican precinct committee positions. Some of these efforts are visible in Arizona.

Most interesting is the story of several Christian Right activists in Arizona who looked at the precinct situation as an opportunity to change the character of what is perceived to be a moderate and libertarian bent to the state's Republican Party. After becoming precinct chairs, they discovered at a district committee meeting that there were forty precincts just in their congressional district that had no committees, let alone chairs. Through their positions as precinct chairs they were able to obtain the "walking lists" for all the precincts in their district. These are the lists of all the people in the district who voted in the previous Republican primary. These lists allow party leaders to identify sympathetic voters on which to concentrate their Get Out the Vote efforts. These Christian Right activists took these lists and walked their own district looking for conservative, pro-life voters. They then encouraged the people they identified to become active in the Republican Party by serving in precinct leadership positions. They believe that because of their efforts, the current majority of the precinct committee people in their district are pro-life. This is in contrast to a more moderate leadership cadre, but their presence has pushed the party in the district to the right.

Observers believe that many efforts like this are thwarted by the basic libertarianism of the Republican Party and general liberalism in the state. Thus, the Christian Right movement is able to achieve some access to the Republican Party, but not enough to change the character of the party from the ground up. The openness and weakness of the party that allows the movement access to precinct committees allows that opening to other groups as well. And, unlike Missouri, the conflictual character of Arizona politics means that there are nonconservative groups seeking the same party access. These difficulties in securing majorities of grassroots support within the party also translate into an inability to help direct the Republican Party through its leadership cadre.

Arizona's Republican Party is rent by internal party division based on a variety of factions. The Republican Party has trouble acting coherently, raising money, or hiding internal conflict from the press. One of the causes for the weakness identified in Arizona's Republican Party is a lack of ideological coherence; the party does not really know what it is. And observers say conflict among the different perspectives exacerbates this identity crisis and tends to fragment Republicans in the state. One observer notes, "Republican success depends on how well this coalition holds. And it depends on the candidate or issue whether it does hold."

Arizona has three or four identifiable factions in its Republican Party. Beyond the standard divisions between business and social conservatives, libertarians and Mormons have a significant impact on the identity of the Republican Party in Arizona. Business conservatives are primarily concerned with population and business growth in the state. The decline in indigenous business in the state has caused concern over the ability of Arizona to control its own destiny. Observers of all stripes comment that this lack of older, more established business leaders can be seen in the lack of social structure underpinning the party. Says one, "Further, there's no indigenous industry anymore. The banks are gone, the cattlemen are gone, the mines are gone, the cotton growers are leaving, Gannett owns the Republic now. There aren't any big companies based in Phoenix, so there isn't the social structure provided by long-term business leaders either. So, whatever social structure there actually was before the growth started is gone now too."

New business leaders want to make sure that the state provides a good climate for business growth as well as providing an educated workforce with the incentive to stay in Arizona. This translates not only into a focus on business issues at the expense of the issues important to social conservatives, but in some cases, direct opposition to the goals of social conservatives. Observers believe that there are more openly gay Republican leaders in the party in Arizona than in any other state in the country. This impacts the way the party views issues such as discrimination and homosexual marriage. Thus, in order to make Arizona as competitive as possible for business growth, most business conservatives are fairly moderate to liberal on social issues like abortion and stem cell research.

The second primary grouping within the Arizona Republican fold is the libertarian faction. The libertarians represent the Arizona version of a significant trend in the western United States toward a preference for very small, unrestrictive government. This sentiment has had a tangible impact on the structure of state government in Arizona as well. Observers say the "Wild West" ethic of the state gives historical grounding to the libertarian movement, while contemporary political developments have nurtured the movement to a solid place at the Republican table. One notes, "People still think of Arizona as the frontier, as the Wild West. This has an impact on how people see themselves here." The presence of a significant libertarian faction in the party has blocked some of the influence the Christian Right might be able to achieve in Arizona's Republican Party leadership structure.

On the other side of the Republican Party are the social, primarily religious, conservatives. Depending on the individual's perspective, this group is seen by observers as either monolithic in its goals and strategies, or rent from within by theological divisions. It seems there is some evidence for a perspective more in line with the latter. While it is certainly the case that on most policy issues, Evangelical and Mormon Republicans seek the same outcomes and work to achieve those, this cooperation has not always been evident within the Republican Party structure itself. The Christian Right side of the movement has split primarily on leadership grounds. Each group wants one of their own to lead the movement. Because Evangelicals are more numerous, they have prevailed in some of these situations, at least within the party. The perception of observers is that the groups' approach politics very differently as well. Evangelicals are more diverse than Mormons, so churches are less involved than they might be if there were more agreement on means and ends. Mormons, on the other hand, are perceived to be more unified ideologically, and this gives them influence because they are more able to mobilize parishioners to behave in ways the leadership approves. While the differences between Evangelicals and Mormons may not yet be significant enough to register outside of Republican circles, the growth of both groups has the potential to cause a significant rift in the social conservative side of the Republican Party in Arizona. One foreshadowing of such future conflict may be demonstrated in the lack of support Matt Salmon, the Republican gubernatorial candidate in 2002, received from Evangelicals. Observers believe that the lack of enthusiasm, and thus voter turnout, demonstrated by Evangelicals in this race was a product of Salmon's Mormon faith. One observer notes, "There was Matt Salmon, who was a Republican gubernatorial candidate and a Mormon. There were Evangelical Christians, Christian Conservatives who wouldn't vote for him because he was Mormon. There were people who actually told him that out on the trail and I think there was some evidence of that out there. So there isn't a full bridge there between those groups."

Arizona has had a unique set of circumstances over the last few years that have increased the polarization of the factions within the Republican Party. One example brings the conflicts into high relief. A Washington DC group called "Club for Growth," an antitax, pro-deregulation group, targeted Arizona as a place to defeat "moderate and liberal" Republicans for state and local offices. The Club drew support from all factions within the Republican Party, business, libertarian, and Christian Right. Many in these factions agree on the need for an economic environment that is as free from regulation as possible. And many of these people supported the Club with donations. Then Steve May, the Club's Arizona director and an openly gay Republican activist, was fired due to opposition from social conservatives and the Christian Right. The Center for Arizona politics sent out a message to its supporters asking them to voice their opposition to May and to tell the Club that they would no longer donate money if a gay activist was in charge in Arizona. This infuriated the business and libertarian factions in the Republican Party. The chairman of the Goldwater Institute, the main venue for libertarian ideas in the state, had suggested

May for the job and felt his firing was a reversal of the freedom for which Club for Growth stood. This ignited conflict between libertarians and social conservatives in the party.[6]

The outgrowth of this situation was a concerted effort by moderate Republicans in response to Club for Growth. Mainstream Arizona was a group of moderate Republicans who set themselves up in opposition to the libertarian and Christian Right factions within the Republican Party. So, they opposed both the policy positions of the Club—describing the Club's actions as outside interference into Arizona politics—and used the leadership controversy as an example of the problems inherent in the more conservative side of the Republican Party. While the Club for Growth was ostensibly its target, Mainstream Arizona continued to operate after the Club pulled out of Arizona. Mainstream Arizona sought a more centrist set of policies and candidates for Arizona. Their claims to be more representative of average voters in Arizona seem to be born out by the recent success of centrist Democrats. Mainstream Arizona disbanded in early 2005 after allegations of campaign finance violations.[7] Given the ideological character of much of this controversy, Arizona provides a good example of how ideological coalitions can significantly constrain the ability of the Christian Right movement to influence Republican politics in a state.

Arizona's party weakness has also shaped the influence of individual personalities on the state and on Republican politics. One cannot discuss Republican politics, let alone Libertarians, in Arizona without mentioning Barry Goldwater. The father of the modern conservative movement, Goldwater is, for all intents and purposes, a libertarian rather than a conservative. His shadow is long in Arizona and few Republicans can escape his legacy. His role came to forefront of the battle by the Christian Right to change abortion policy in Arizona in 1992. A referendum intended to outlaw most forms of abortion in the state was defeated after Goldwater made and broadcast television commercials in opposition to the referendum. Thus there is a significant strain of antiregulation libertarianism that tends to thwart the goals of the Christian Right in the state. The libertarian faction and the business faction tend to either overlap or partner on many issues to encourage free enterprise and discourage social regulations.

In contemporary Arizona politics, John McCain dominates the Republican Party and its strategies. While he tends to ignore the party organization itself, concentrating on his own campaigns and national politics, he is the polestar for Republican conversation in the state. McCain is a very moderate Republican, who tends toward the middle in economic issues and libertarianism in social issues. Republican observers point out that many Arizona Republicans of all stripes refuse to claim him, citing the fact that his primary base of support is among independents and moderate Democrats. But others hold him up as a good example of how Republicans should behave. Clearly, McCain is opposed to the Christian Right philosophy—his attempts at reconciliation during 2008 presidential campaign notwithstanding—and so his presence is a polarizing factor in the state. Interestingly, while many more conservative Republicans would like to challenge McCain's dominance, he seems to be too well respected and funded in the larger state for the call for change to get much notice. Further, he is perceived to be closer in opinions to business conservatives and most of them are content to allow him to retain his office. He is certainly effective in convincing voters that his seniority in the Senate is a benefit for Arizona. But his overwhelming and polarizing presence has helped to keep the party weak because they do not fully embrace him as one of their own.

The Republican Party's inherent weakness, the division of internal factions, and the availability of Clean Elections campaign money outside of the party purview have created a situation where the Republican Party is ineffectual in much of what it tries to accomplish. Further, it has set up a situation where there is a significant disconnect between grassroots supporters and party leadership. It has been very difficult for the Christian Right to translate its significant numbers of Evangelical constituents into party power, and thus they have turned to other, more effective means of changing public policy.

## THE CHRISTIAN RIGHT IN
## LEGISLATIVE POLITICS IN ARIZONA

Paralleling the political party system in Arizona, state laws seem designed to make the legislature as weak as possible and still be able to function as government. Legislators serve under term limits and their decisions are subject to a popular referenda law that makes it quite easy for citizens to overturn the legislature's decisions. These characteristics tend to produce a situation where the party caucuses have less power to convince members to vote together than they might in other states. This combined with a Democratic governor have made the Christian Right's success rate fairly low in the Arizona legislature over the last several years, but that is certainly not for lack of trying. The movement seems to use the legislature as its primary way of working around the Republican Party. However, the lack of strength and organization in Arizona's Republican Party disadvantages the movement in the legislature as well. Without a strong party organization to push compliance and unity, any group seeking to influence policy making in legislative politics, or state politics in general, has a disadvantage. This party weakness is further exacerbated by a governmental system in Arizona that has traditionally been thought of as weak, and a set of state institutional mores that assume that this state of affairs is a good thing.

Arizona's government is set up in such a way as to significantly limit its power. Observers believe that the legislature is old-fashioned, weak, and underpaid. It is certainly an amateur body, meeting only 123 days a year and being paid $24,000 a year. The executive branch's power is limited as well, with fewer elected officials than average and no lieutenant governor. This general government weakness translates into a situation where policy coordination is difficult because of weaker central authority. It is clear that the citizens of Arizona originally desired and continue to desire a government that does not intrude into their personal lives. This system is problematic for all groups who seek policy change in the state, not just the Christian Right. The weakness of the government limits the scope of public policy in the state. Financial and time constraints limit the amount of legislation that can be passed and implemented and Arizona lacks Indiana's interim study committees. So groups are competing for scarce regulatory resources in addition to trying to convince legislators to implement favored policies. Again, this challenges the Christian Right movement as it tries to work around a weak Republican Party using a weak legislature.

Since 2000, members of the legislature are limited to eight years of service in each house. As in many states, term limits seem to have strengthened the power of outside groups in Arizona politics. As legislators need to rely on lobbyists and interest group leaders for policy and bill information, these actors gain in strength and influence over policy making. This has worked both as a benefit and a barrier to Christian Right influence in the state legislature. This situation is a benefit to those movement groups who are active in their attempts to influence legislators. It becomes a barrier though, when groups or individuals opposed to the Christian Right's agenda become active and gain access in the state. Both of these situations have occurred in Arizona, with some legislators relying heavily on the Center for Arizona Politics and others situating themselves in strong opposition to the group. It appears that this is because there seems to be a wider range of opinions represented in the state legislature than in many other states. It is possible that this situation is due to the state's attractiveness as a relocation spot, altering what might be a "natural" level of policy opinion homogeneity.

Like Arizona's Republican Party, the Republican caucuses in the state legislature are rent by internal ideological disputes, making it a challenge for the movement to work around the party using the legislature. One observer describes it as, "Conservatives control the leadership of the Republican Party in the legislature; they have the caucus, but there are enough moderates that they can cut outside deals with the Democratic minority to get things done. There is no discipline in the caucus . . . The moderates in the House aren't facing primary opposition, so they'll continue their revolt." This situation is further complicated by the fact that the Christian Right and their policy positions have produced strong opposition from both more liberal Republican factions and most of the Democrats in the legislature. The strong presence of Mormons in the state legislature and Republican leadership complicates matters for the Christian Right even further. While less than 10 percent of the state's population is Mormon, observers say that most of the Republican leadership in both houses are LDS. In fact, it is clear that when some commentators are asked about the Christian Right movement in the state, they think primarily of these Mormon office holders, not others more traditionally in line with the Christian Right—primarily Evangelical—movement and its organizations. As in other venues of Republican politics in Arizona, Christian Right groups tend to have some tension in their relationship with these Mormon legislators. And because the Mormon legislators seem to focus on their own church contacts instead of Christian Right activists for information, there tends to be a lack of communication and coordination between the two groups.

More so than in other states in this study, groups in opposition to the Christian Right have an impact on state politics in Arizona. This presents a significant challenge to movement activists as they try to influence state policy. In many states, most Republicans are, if not Christian Right supporters themselves, amenable to the movements' issue positions and retain close ties to movement representatives, both legislators and lobbyists. This is less the case in Arizona. There is a fairly large, observable group of Republicans in the legislature that is generally opposed to the Christian Right's social agenda. These Republicans represent both moderate and libertarian factions in the party. Further, the Arizona legislature has the highest percentage of openly gay legislators in the country who are represented on both sides of the aisle. These characteristics present a demonstrable problem for the movement in Arizona. Observers and activists believe it is these Republicans who are most detrimental to the movements' efforts particularly on abortion regulation and the repeal of sodomy laws in 2001.

Mirroring their role in state Christian Right politics overall, the Center for Arizona Policy is the largest player in Christian Right lobbying in the Arizona legislature and has seen its activity increase since the advent of term limits, according to observers. The Center wrote the defense of marriage law that was enacted by Arizona in 1996 and a wide variety of other pro-family bills that have been considered or passed. This is a primary example of the growing influence of Christian Rights made possible by legislators' need for information and policy support services. One observer notes that the Center has strategic friends in the legislature and can get some bills killed or gutted in committee if need be. The observer further believes that the Center works like all other political interests when they are lobbying, they use all the same strategies and tactics to stall or pass legislation.

Thus, the movement, through the Center for Arizona Policy, is active in lobbying and providing legislative services to like-minded members of the legislature. The Christian Right's problem in Arizona, however, is that there seem to be too few like-minded legislators to serve. The movement has been active in legislative races, particularly because it is very easy to run such campaigns outside the purview of the Republican Party, but the unique demographics of the state have proved challenging to the movement's ability to elect sympathetic Republicans. The vast majority of the population is concentrated in the Phoenix area, robbing the movement of the rural support that is so decisive in many other states. There is very little rural population in Arizona because the climate and landscape do little to support scattered populations. Phoenix itself is somewhat segregated in terms of the characteristics of its population as well. Observers say that Mormons tend to congregate in particular geographic areas, like Mesa in the East Valley, and that retirees, who tend to vote Republican but who do not necessarily support Christian Right policy issues, tend to congregate in the newer towns west of the city. These concentrations of similar individuals make it difficult for Christian Right supporters to play the critical role at the margins of elections as they do in many other states.[8]

This is particularly the case when, as observers note, perhaps 80 percent of state legislative races are decided in the primary because of a lack of credible general election opponents. While the Republican Party enjoys a registration majority in the state and the House and Senate have been controlled by Republicans for the last several years, many observers point to the fact that Republicans are generally more moderate in Arizona than in other places. So, while overall Republican victories have brought more Christian Right supporters in the state legislature, the even larger proportion of moderate Republicans has largely marginalized these Christian Right legislators who are seen as ultraconservative. Thus, the Christian Right works to be successful in electing legislators from areas with higher concentrations of sympathetic voters, but these may be too small to give the movement the kind of support it needs in the legislature.

Thus, the almost uniquely varied makeup of the Arizona legislature, combined with term limits, creates an environment with both significant opportunity and significant challenges for Christian Right activists. The movement seems to achieve influence when it can join or create coalitions around particular issues. But the presence of significant opposition factions in the legislature makes this difficult. The movement is certainly seeking to work around the party in many cases, but find any success difficult in a state with such a wide range of viewpoints in opposition to the movement's social conservatism.

One of these avenues for policy influence is the power for citizen instigated ballot initiative and referenda. Based on law and precedent, citizens in Arizona utilize these methods more often than do citizens in Missouri, and this is reflected in the way the Christian Right approach initiatives and referenda in the two states. Arizona has had more than three times the number of initiatives make the ballot as Missouri, even though both states instituted the method at approximately the same time (1907 for Missouri, 1912 for Arizona).

In Arizona, the use of the ballot initiative is widespread and is understood as an important part of the fabric of politics in the state. As noted throughout this case study, there is a significant ethic of citizen government in Arizona. Thus, there is an understanding that the voters of the state have as much right to make laws as do their representatives in the legislature. One observer noted that the legislature is careful about the types of bills it passes because they know that if people in the state are unhappy with their actions, citizens will initiate the popular referendum process to change the law. "In Arizona, people don't trust the legislature. They tend to use the initiative and referenda to bypass the legislature." Another observer called it "an end run around the legislature." Thus, it is clear that there is significant and widespread precedent for the use of the referendum and the ballot initiative in Arizona. This use of the initiative and referendum is so widespread because state laws provide for easy access to the process. Arizonans are permitted to propose initiatives on any topic and the number of signatures required is relatively low. Further, it takes a ¾ supermajority in the legislature to overturn any citizen initiated action.

The Christian Right in Arizona has used the ballot initiative and referenda processes to work around the Republican Party in the state. While there have been a number of proposed initiatives that failed to make the ballot, two successful efforts stand out as examples of how the movement has used the initiative and referendum process to try work around the party. In neither case did the efforts succeed, proving again that the state as a whole does not share the social conservatism of the Christian Right. In an attempt to outlaw abortion in the state without requiring support from the Republican Party leadership, in 1992 the movement introduced an initiative that outlawed abortion in most cases and gathered enough signatures to place it on the ballot. The effort failed, but the movement learned that the initiative process was available to them as a means for changing social policy.[9]

Spearheaded by the Center for Arizona Politics, the Christian Right gathered enough signatures to place an initiative on the ballot in the fall of 2006 to amend the state constitution and define marriage as between one man and one woman. Following the success of such initiatives in thirteen states in 2004, the Christian Right in Arizona saw an opening to significantly alter public policy. Movement organizations worked hard to gather signatures, sending their supporters a barrage of e-mails making sure they knew where to go to sign the petitions and encouraging them to ask their friends to sign as well. The campaign to pass the amendment was fierce with Christian Right activists claiming that the measure took the issue out of the courts' hands—its greatest worry following decisions by the Supreme Courts of Massachusetts and New Jersey. Cathi Herrod, spokesperson for Protect Marriage Arizona, was quoted in the *Arizona Republic*, "If we don't add a definition of marriage to the Arizona Constitution, it is a matter of time before Arizona judges redefine marriage through our court."[10] But the ballot measure failed, 51.4 percent to 48.6 percent. Polls suggested that the defeat came in part because the amendment also denied benefits to all unmarried couples and was perceived as impinging on individual rights.[11] Though the movement claimed the defeat was due to misinformation from their opponents, the results suggests once again that the Christian Right is not in the mainstream of Arizona politics, and it pays the price even when it is able to work around both the Republican Party and the state legislature in its quest to make more conservative social policy.

The Christian Right faces numerous challenges in Arizona. The movement seems to have great difficulty achieving its policy goals whether through the state's Republican Party, the state legislature, or popular initiatives and referenda. What separates Arizona's Christian Right from those state movements discussed later in Chapter 7 is the presence of avenues for policy influence, limited though they may be. The possibility for change remains as the structure of state and party politics and the inherent vitality of the movement give the Christian Right the ingredients for possible success. The movement has not given up in Arizona; it is not "going home." But it faces challenges as it continually seeks to make state policy more amenable to their values.

## WORKING WITHIN AND WORKING AROUND WITH LIMITED SUCCESS

Arizona's political opportunity structure has created a situation where the Christian Right seeks both to work within and work around the party. The movement's primary goal is to shape public policy in ways that best fit its cultural and theological view points. Arizona is a great example of how the movement adapts to the realities of its context and seeks policy changes in whatever ways are available. The movement has been somewhat successful in the grassroots portion of the Republican Party and has had a few of its ranks accede to party leadership, but overall, the strength of the moderate and libertarian faction in the party, combined with the uncertain status of Mormon conservatives, has made it difficult for the Christian Right to utilize the party in the way it would wish. While the movement has had some success in working around the party in political campaigns, it has also sought to work directly with Republicans in the legislature to achieve its goals. In many ways, the movement faces similar problems in the state legislature, with moderate forces opposing its positions and a conflicted relationship with Mormon legislative leadership complicating its efforts. Finally, though taking advantage of the liberal opportunities for popular ballot initiative and referenda usage, the Christian Right has been defeated in its major attempts to use this political tool. Overall, while the movement itself exhibits vitality and grassroots appeal in certain areas, the overall libertarian and individual-rights orientation of the vast majority of Arizona's population has made the Christian Right's policy orientation a persistent minority in state politics.

The uniqueness of the situation in Arizona bolsters my theory because the Christian Right behaves in the ways the theory would predict. It uses the openings available in the Republican Party and works around the party when it needs to. These strategic decisions are based on the movement's response to the political opportunity structure, internal resources, and threat mobilization situation it faces. The strategy of the Arizona Christian Right is affected by state laws governing party behavior in a number of ways. The state mandated September primaries provide low interest elections that the movement can utilize in their favor by increasing turnout. And party law governs the number of precincts and party committees up the leadership chain, making the system transparent to the movement. Most importantly the Clean Elections law makes it very easy for candidates for all state offices to run outside the purview of the party. This has been a double edged sword for the movement, removing power from the Republican Party that could be used by the movement in situations of party dominance, but also allowing the Christian Right to work around the party and work for the election of likeminded politicians. Further, the high incidence of uncontested general elections makes activities in the primaries even more fruitful for the movement.

The resources available to the Christian Right movement in Arizona allow the movement to actively pursue its policy goals even in the face of general policy weakness in the state. With a large proportion of Evangelicals in the state, the movement has a natural grassroots base from which to work. While the presence of a significant minority of Mormons complicates the movement's strategies at higher levels, the grassroots activism of Mormons is generally in the same policy direction as the Christian Right. These strengths allow the movement to take advantage of the openings available both within the Republican Party and in the larger political system. The Christian Right network is well developed, and there is significant evidence that activists from different issue areas are willing and able to work together under the auspices of the Center for Arizona Politics. This cohesion is certainly assisted by the societal threat social conservatives of all stripes feel in Arizona's Wild West culture.

In many other states, this internal movement strength combined with the structural openings in the system would provide the movement with great success. The Christian Right is certainly active and playing a part in Arizona politics. But as this chapter has shown, the movement is significantly hampered by the libertarian and moderate factions within Republican politics and a general opposition to social control in the larger population. Arizona proves to be a good example of the way the Christian Right adapts itself to the political context in which it finds itself. Playing on its suburban grassroots strength, the movement makes a difference where it can, in the precinct levels of the Republican Party, in popular ballot initiatives and referenda, and by combining its resources into a single steering organization. The Center for Arizona Politics provides the locus of power outside the party from which the movement operates. This strategy has served the Christian Right as well as it can; giving the movement a voice, but limited impact on the public policy of Arizona.

# CHAPTER 7

---◆◆◆◆---

# GOING HOME, BUT NOT GIVING UP

Unfriendly party leadership; arcane party bylaws; legislative gridlock. As we have seen, these can all prove to be significant barriers to Christian Right political action. But sometimes, these barriers prove to be insurmountable. The stakes are high for Christian Right activists. They seek long term influence in the policy-making decisions of state parties and politics. If they fail, the movement can keep trying, expending time, money, and effort to overcome failure, or the movement can just cease to seek influence at all; they can "go home." While evidence suggests that this is fairly rare, it does seem to be the case that the Christian Right movement can be too weak to overcome the structural barriers to influencing public policy in a particular state. The movement can be thwarted by a party that is closed to it, a professionalized or unsympathetic legislative branch, or a lack of citizen access to government decisions. In some cases, a new issue or threat will emerge in a state, and latent movement support will emerge, only to be crushed by the political realities of too few Evangelicals and too few political opportunities. When this happens, the Christian Right concentrates on other, nonpolitical methods of impacting the society in which they live.

Observing what happens in situations where the movement has chosen to go home is a challenge for a variety of reasons. Primarily the problem is one of focus. Researchers generally pay attention to the presence of an attribute or phenomenon, not its absence. Thus, while states where the movement is strong have been studied in depth, little research has focused on those states exhibiting little Christian Right influence. Even this project, focusing as it does on states previously unobserved for movement activity, looks almost entirely at situations where the movement is demonstrably active, not silent. Thus the data I offer for this chapter may be less concrete than the other chapters. But it should provide a story with face validity that opens news avenues for further research on the phenomenon.

While the concept of "going home" operates like the other analytical categories in this analysis—on the level of the whole movement being thwarted in its attempt to influence state public policy—individuals can decide to go home as well, even in situations where the movement has had some success. Individual activists can be overwhelmed by the obstacles inherent in trying to change public policy. This is particularly likely in social movement situations like the ones I am studying. With no centralized structure to coordinate effort, individuals may underestimate their strength due to lack of knowledge of others' efforts. Thus, in this chapter, I examine both types of going home; generalized, systemwide withdrawal in states where the movement has little impact, and individual retreats in states where the movement has had success.

## Saying Goodbye

The Christian Right decides not to seek influence through political means based on the same strategic calculations that lead them to either work within or work around the Republican Party in their state. Political opportunity structure, movement resources, and threat mobilization; for the purposes of this chapter, we can think of these in two categories: closed institutions and weak movements. In many ways, these characteristics simply work in the opposite direction of their effects on activists in states where the movement has some level of success. In states where the Christian Right goes home, activists are thwarted by state laws that limit citizen participation, by an internal party structure that protects the organization from insurgencies, and by the internal characteristics of the movement itself, usually weakness and lack of support. To clarify, it is not that one of these avenues to influence is closed to the movement. If that were the case, movements would proceed to work around that rule or institution as they do with political parties. The kind of situation that causes the Christian Right to go home is one where all of these methods of influencing policy are closed to activists. Generally speaking, there are a group of factors working against the movement, not simply one closed institution. A closer look at each of these areas will provide a more comprehensive picture of the dynamics surrounding a state Christian Right movement that goes home.

First, Christian Right activists may face a situation in a state where the structures of political institutions are closed to them. The Republican Party is closed to their influence through state law or party rules that set up difficult barriers for activists to move into party leadership or to influence party decision-making functions such as the state committee or party platform. In cases where the movement goes home, however, there are no avenues available to work around the party. The institutional structures of the other influence options are closed to them as well. In these states, the legislature is closed to the movement, primarily because there are few sympathetic members to help support movement legislation. This can be exacerbated by a lack of term limits and an operating procedure that favors private decision making among powerful legislators. When the movement is blocked from using the party or the legislature, they generally turn to the ballot initiative, referenda, and the courts.

However, avenues for direct citizen impact on lawmaking are only available in half the states. Generally speaking, the availability of these modes of influence is related to the statutory openness of the political parties. Many of the reforms put in place to make parties more open to citizen involvement mirrored efforts to make all government decisions transparent to the public. Thus open party systems tend to go hand in hand with the ability to use ballot initiative and referenda, and vice versa. So, a movement that has difficulty impacting a state's Republican Party because of the way the organization is structured will likely face a situation where they have no recourse through citizen decision making. We see this happening in states like Indiana where the progressive movement and its reforms had little impact on the state's parties or politics. As described in Chapter 4, however, the movement has been very successful in the state legislature, thus obviating the need to control the party.

The courts are generally the movement's last resort in a state. Again, state judicial elections tend to be tied to open political parties and citizen decision making due to Progressive Era reforms. So, in states where the Christian Right finds itself without an entry to the party and no way of influencing state policy through ballot initiatives or referenda, it is likely that the option of seeking to elect state judges will also be closed. So that leaves the movement's only hope in challenging state laws with which they disagree as litigation in the state court system. Obviously, the outcome of such a strategy will depend on the personnel and philosophy of the courts. If these are opposed to the movement, then the last chance is removed.

The previous discussion is a logical outcome of the earlier chapters of this book. If the conditions for the movement's ability to successfully influence public policy at the state level are not met, the movement cannot have influence. But going home seems to be one step further in reaction to this lack of opportunity for influence. In some states, the movement is thwarted at every turn; it has basically no success in trying to change the policy or politics of the state. Yet, movement activists continue to organize, raise money, and seek awareness for their issues. So, they are demonstrably not going home.

New York seems to be a reasonable case of this. With a Democratically controlled state legislature, public opinion that is generally skewed to the liberal end of the political spectrum, a Republican Party that is closed to the movement's influence both in organizational terms and ideological coalition, and no ballot initiative or referenda powers, the movement seems to have no ability to impact state politics. Yet, activists continue to seek influence. The state has a Family Research Council Affiliate and even a pro-life political party through which movement activists work.[1] So, clearly, there is a key difference between states like New York and states where the movement has gone home. My assertion is that the difference is based on internal movement resources, primarily the number of Evangelicals the movement has to draw on for support in a given state.

We see in many cases where the movement has gone home that there are very few Evangelicals in the state. This suggests that there may be a threshold of activism below which the Christian Right movement cannot sustain itself. While it seems likely that this threshold is low—there are few states in which the movement exhibits no activity at all—but it can be the primary factor affecting a movement's decision to go home, particularly in states with difficult to access systems where numbers of supporters matter to a greater degree.

There are Evangelical Christians in every state in the Union. However, there are states where their numbers are very small. This is particularly true in the Northeast. In states where there are few Evangelicals, the Christian Right has few resources to draw on for support. Evangelicals are the primary constituency of the movement, and without these religiously conservative people in a state, the movement finds few supporters. Even though other religious groups may hold Christian Right policy preferences, Evangelicals really form the core of the activist base. Because the Christian Right is a social movement, it needs a wide range of people to exert influence on society and government to change public policy. In fact, without a number of such supporters, the movement never really gets off the ground. So the number of Evangelicals in a state is vital to the movement's ability to even begin to seek influence in a state's politics. In most states, the numbers of Evangelicals are enough to mount some type of movement, however small. However, in a few states, the movement cannot muster enough supporters even in a few geographic areas to even seek societal change.

This internal weakness may also be brought about by internal divisions, where factions within the movement disagree over ideology or tactics, or by a leadership vacuum. Evidence suggests that while these situations are possible, they are less likely to cause the movement to go home than a simple lack of supporters. Divisions are less costly when the movement has enough supporters to disseminate influence to a wide variety of venues and leadership vacuums are typically short-lived if there are openings within the state's institutional structures for the movement to make impact with coordinated effort. So while these situations are theoretically possible, they are unlikely in the present American context.

A good example of this type of lack of Evangelical population is Vermont. Only about 5 percent of the population consider themselves to be observant Evangelicals, while 32 percent of the population consider themselves to be secular. There are very few observant believers of any faith in the state and almost 60 percent of the population has a negative view of the Christian Right.[2] Vermont exhibits a very low level of Christian Right influence in its state Republican Party.[3] Evidence suggests the movement has gone home in Vermont. In 2000, the state legislature passed a law legalizing civil unions for same-sex couples in the state after Vermont's Supreme Court had mandated that the state must provide legal recognition for homosexual relationships. Most of the opposition to the measure came from groups from outside the state. The single homegrown effort died out as it became clear that the Republican Party, the legislature, and the courts supported the measure and that local ballot initiatives (the only legal venue for citizen lawmaking in the state) would be impossible to pass due to widespread support for civil unions in Vermont.[4] Thus the Christian Right sought to influence public policy in Vermont, to repeal the civil union law, and was completely thwarted by the political opportunity structure in which it found itself and by its lack of movement resources. Given that Christian Right supporters initially attempted to get the measure repealed, one can wonder how far the effort might have gone with more Evangelicals and other religiously conservative supporters in the state.

As we can see in Vermont and other states like it, the Christian Right movement is thwarted at every turn in its desire to change public policy. The combination of closed political institutions and a small number of potential supporters makes it impossible for the movement to have any impact on state politics and so activists go home, and seek nonpolitical ways of changing the society around them. It is not a single state characteristic that causes the movement to withdraw, but the whole universe of state politics arrayed against it. Vermont is also a good example of the determinative role that grassroots support has in allowing the Christian Right movement to continue activity in the face of opposition or to withdraw. In a state where observant Evangelicals make up less than 5 percent of the population, the movement simply lacks the resources to overcome the structural (and ideological) obstacles to its ability to change public policy. But in these states where the movement has decided to go home, that withdrawal is usually not forever. Institutional and movement contexts can change over time, persuading activists to try again to influence public policy. In many states we can observe cyclical withdrawal, where the movement may mount another effort due to new issues or activists. But structural factors and low numbers of Evangelicals tend to remain constant over time, making going home a recurring phenomenon.

## CYCLES OF ACTIVITY

Because the context in which activists find themselves changes over time, so do the strategic calculations of movement activists as they seek to impact public policy in their state. Generally speaking, these changes in context affect the perceived stakes of activity, not the institutional structural situation the movement faces. These changes in context include new activists and new issues that arise and change the level of threat perceived by Christian Right supporters in a state. New activists arise through generational replacement. As new Christian Right supporters become politically aware and active, they are more likely to seek influence in state politics because they have no experience being personally rebuffed by a closed political system. Also, it is clear from other research that new generations of activist use different tactics and perceive themselves to have learned from the past failures of the Christian Right movement.[5] It also seems to be the case, particularly in states with few Evangelicals and a moribund Christian Right movement, that outside or national groups seek to mobilize what support they can for policy initiatives. It may be the efforts of these groups that foster newer activists to try again to impact politics.

The other evolution in political context that may produce cycles of Christian Right activity is the emergence of new hot-button issues in state politics. These types of issues, usually social or moral in nature, have the potential to increase the level of threat that Christian Right supporters perceive in their social and political environment. As we have seen in earlier chapters, movement activists' level of motivation seems to be linked to the level of threat they feel within their state context. So, the introduction of new social legislation, such as a freer abortion license or the legalization of same-sex marriage, tends to greatly increase the level of threat that religious conservatives perceive. This increase in perception of threat changes the strategic calculus of activists as they approach state politics. Because they feel the stakes are higher than in the past, they are more likely to seek influence even if they have been rebuffed or gone home before. Again, activists may continue to operate in a closed political system, however, and their efforts may lead to cyclical failure. Massachusetts provides an interesting example in prominent public issues affecting the level of threat perceived by the movement.

In November, 2003, the Supreme Court of Massachusetts ruled that the state's constitution prohibited officials from denying marriage licenses to same-sex couples. In that decision, the court gave the Massachusetts legislature six months to rewrite state law to reflect their ruling. The legislature failed to do so, and a proposed constitutional amendment that banned same-sex marriage but permitted civil unions failed to receive enough support. Same-sex marriages have been taking place in the state since mid-2004. Another constitutional amendment campaign was launched by the Christian Right affiliated Massachusetts Family Institute in 2004. With help from the national Family Research Council, the group was able to collect the required number of signatures to place the amendment before the constitutional convention. While the convention passed the amendment, a number of court cases are pending to determine the legality of the means by which it reached the convention. Currently, legislative wrangling and the uncertain status of the constitutional amendment make the future of same-sex marriage in Massachusetts unclear.

Massachusetts is a state with an even smaller proportion of observant Evangelicals than Vermont.[6] Long a bastion of liberal Democratic politics, the state has a Republican Party that is generally opposed to Christian Right viewpoints and a professionalized state legislature with significant structural and ideological opposition to the movement. This is not a state where one would imagine the movement to have significant power. Yet, the threat to the moral fabric of society perceived by Christian Right supporters and religious conservatives with the advent of same-sex marriage in the state dramatically changed the strategic choices of the movement. The Vote on Marriage project has collected a record number of signatures on the petitions to put the marriage amendment before the constitutional convention. While the movement is clearly getting support from non-Evangelical conservatives, it is also clear that Christian Right activists are spearheading this movement. If they are successful in changing the state's constitution, it could signal a real sea change in the movement's prospects in the state. But it is important to point out that the movement would not have had this opportunity had Massachusetts not had legal provisions for citizens to offer constitutional amendments. Again, we see the importance of political opportunity structure in shaping and constraining the ability of the Christian Right movement to change public policy. If the movement is unsuccessful, however, it will demonstrate the validity of my theory that when all political forces are arrayed against Christian Rights in a state with few movement resources, the movement has little choice but to retreat and go home.

## THE ROLE OF OPPOSITION

As we have noted in states where the Christian Right has gone home, political opposition to the movement and its goals can play a significant part in the movement's decision making. In the Northeast, this is most clearly demonstrated in a general policy liberalism that is a feature of both mass and elite public opinion. Clearly, the low numbers of Evangelicals is correlated with this policy liberalism, but the overall tenor of state politics is such that the movement feels opposition from individuals and groups whenever it seeks to influence public policy. Thus opposition in states where there are few Evangelicals can operate in two ways. The general content of public opinion may be against the movement. This will affect the characteristics of the elected officials in the state, and will indirectly affect public policy as lawmakers make decisions they see as consonant with the general will. Opposition to the Christian Right and its policy agenda may also exist both within the Republican Party and among government officials in general. Opponents in these positions can make a hard situation even harder for the movement. As we have seen, the ability of movement activists to make inroads into the Republican Party is greatly affected by the ideological coalitions within the party. Widespread personal opposition alters the balance of power in that coalition and makes it impossible for the Christian Right to have an impact.

Opposition to the movement within the party is certainly instrumental in shaping the Christian Right in Arizona. The large number of libertarians in the Republican Party makes it a hard place for the movement to operate. While the movement has found ways to work around this situation, helped by the large numbers of observant Evangelicals in the state, opposition plays a big role in the state, making it less amenable to Christian Right influence than it might be based purely on institutional structure or movement characteristics.

So while organized opposition does not usually make the difference for the Christian Right in the movement's decision to withdraw from politics in a state, it can have a significant effect on the ability of the movement to move their agenda forward. It is also certainly one of the many forces arrayed against the movement when it does decide to go home. Opposition may also impact a particular type of decision to go home, that of the individual activist. Because the Christian Right is a social movement, activists are not always well connected to one another; individuals may become isolated and find themselves being thwarted in their particular endeavors. These activists may decide on their own to go home; they may burn out and come to the conclusion that they cannot affect public policy through their own efforts.

## ACTIVIST BURNOUT AND GOING HOME

Even in states where the Christian Right has had success in affecting public policy, some individual activists are unable to impact policy or politics on their own terms and tire of seeking influence. In that case they may go home even when the larger movement is working within or around the Republican Party. These individuals may seem to have little to do with our overarching understanding of the ways the Christian Right interacts with the Republican Party and larger politics of their states, but the characteristics of these thwarted activists help us understand the dynamics of change within the movement and how that affects the movement's political prospects over time.

Observers in many states have noted that over time, there are fewer and fewer pastors involved in the movement. It seems that in the early days, particularly the 1980s, there were many Evangelical pastors actively engaged in supporting the movement and encouraging their congregations to follow suit. Over time, their numbers have dwindled as many have concluded that they are more effective at changing society by working through moral and social activism outside of politics, largely through their congregations. This represents a whole group of individuals who have decided to go home, even in states where the movement has had great success. This is true as well in Indiana, Missouri, and Arizona. Many activists expressed to me their desire that their pastors be more involved in politics as they were in the past. It seems likely that these pastors felt that their efforts were not achieving the desired ends. So pastors as a group have gone home due to the opposition they faced and the internal structure of the movement that was not achieving the goals of changing society in a way they could support. Obviously, this is not true for all Evangelical pastors; there are still quite a few at work on political issues. But the perception is that, as a group, pastors are much less involved than they were in the 1980s.

Other individual activists get burned out and go home as well. Social movements have difficulty sustaining the intensity of activists' support over long periods of time. When the movement does not achieve all or even some of its goals, it is much more likely that supporters will tire of the effort and return to their nonpolitical lives. According to observers, this can be seen in some of the activism surrounding the prevention of abortion. In the past, people that one would consider to be normal or average Evangelicals were likely to take part in pro-life activities, such as picketing abortion clinics. Fewer of this type of supporter are active in this way in the contemporary movement. This is due to the perception that picketing abortion clinics makes one closer to the radical behavior of Randall Terry and Operation Rescue, a group that advocated civil disobedience and even violence in order to prevent abortions. Second, this situation is due to the lack of progress within the abortion issue area over the past thirty-five years. Grassroots pro-life activists tire when they do not perceive that their efforts bear any fruit. Abortion is still legal in the United States and these activists feel thwarted by the political system in which they operate and so they go home.

Thus the Christian Right may be thwarted at every turn both within the structure of political institutions or because of its own internal weaknesses, but individuals can be thwarted enough to retreat as well. In either case the issues come down to the ability of activists to work within the system to change public policy. If they cannot influence public policy, they go home.

## CONCLUSION

What happens when the Christian Right decides to go home in a particular state? The impulse to reform society does not necessarily disappear, it is just not focused toward the political arena anymore. We can see this in the rise of organizations affiliated with the movement that are involved in social action with little political content. Probably the best example of this is Crisis Pregnancy Centers. This is a nonprofit group that operates all over the United States providing abortion counseling and adoption referrals. While not involved in politics directly, the group is directly involved with trying to reduce the number of abortions that occur. Clearly part of the Christian Right social movement, Crisis Pregnancy Centers does not try to change society by changing public policy, but by changing the attitudes and behaviors of individuals within the society. Religious conservatives may also support the Christian Right at the national level through membership and donations. Some supporters find this to be the best alternative to no activity at all.

The Christian Right continues to focus on societal change, regardless of the venue. This aspect of the movement makes it more likely that going home is not forever. Though the movement may be currently unable to influence politics or policy in a particular state, situations change, bringing new opportunities and issues to the fore. The Christian Right is willing and able to embark on these cyclical quests for influence because their underlying motivation, to change society, does not change.

# CHAPTER 8

———◆❈◆———

## PUTTING IT ALL TOGETHER

### STRATEGY AND INFLUENCE ACROSS THE STATES

It all started in Iowa, as many political phenomena do. From unknown status as late as November, 2007, to the convincing winner of the Iowa Republican caucuses on January 3, 2008, Mike Huckabee became the putative "Christian Right" candidate in the 2008 Republican nomination race. His well-known past as a Baptist minister, his open expression of Evangelical faith, and his conservative social views made him a popular candidate among the religious conservative Republican caucus-goers in Iowa. Huckabee went on to win the nomination contests of seven more states, mostly in the South, the heartland of Christian Right support. But Huckabee did not have the unanimous backing of the movement in the way President Bush did in 2004. In fact, most Evangelical and Christian Right leaders supported other candidates. His campaign was a grassroots effort, based in state- and local-level politics, that garnered Huckabee the groundswell of support he received before eventually conceding the race to John McCain. Many have seen in this Republican nomination contest the fragmentation of the Christian Right, and in the general election results of 2008, the end of the Christian Right movement. While that diagnosis may be true in a broad sense, others have seen in the situation a stronger focus on a movement based in the states, not at the national level. Many believe that this means there will never be another national leader who gains the unqualified support from all sectors of the movement. Huckabee did well in many states where the Christian Right is perceived to be strong. Yet McCain did equally well or better in other states with similar numbers of Evangelicals and general conservatism. This highlights the differences across the states in terms of the movement, its goals, its strategies, and its success.

In this chapter we come full circle. The Indiana, Missouri, and Arizona case studies provide evidence that the Christian Right's level of influence and strategy in state-level politics is shaped by its interaction with the Republican Party. Movement activists decide to work within the party, work around it, or go home and not seek influence in a state's politics based on the political opportunity structure they face, the resources the movement brings to the table, and the degree to which threat has mobilized the movement's constituency. In this chapter, we revisit the theory I posited in Chapter 3 and examine how well the case studies demonstrate its usefulness in understanding the Christian Right and its role in state-level Republican politics. Next, I mine the rich vein of qualitative data available on the Christian Right in a wide variety of other states to demonstrate the usefulness of my theory beyond the states examined in this book. Finally, I explore more deeply the relationship between the Christian Right's strategy and its level of influence to bring the book's contribution of applying political process model (PPM) to state-level party politics into clearer focus. Across the board, it is evident that my theory concerning the relationship between the Republican Party and state-level Christian Right activists helps us to understand the wide variations in movement strategy and success that we can observe across the fifty states.

## CASE STUDY CONNECTIONS

As the experiences of the Christian Right in Indiana, Missouri, and Arizona, along with the several states discussed more briefly in Chapter 7, the movement really defines its strategy based on its relationship with the state-level Republican Party. The Christian Right makes the decision to work within the party, to work around it, or go home altogether within the political and social context in which it finds itself. We can use the well-developed literature on the relationship between social movements and their political contexts to help us understand the movement's choices and successes in a theoretically coherent way.

In the political process model, the first set of constraints that mold social movement behavior and success are contained in the political opportunity structure. In this case, the political opportunity structure faced by the Christian Right in state-level Republican politics is made up of the laws and traditions that govern political parties in each state, the wider laws and traditions of the state that shape politics, and the policy process in the state as a whole.

This role for internal party structure is seen clearly in Missouri, where both the formal and informal laws and traditions were supportive of Christian Right entry into the party. Both the generalized conservatism of the party and its leadership, and the distinct need for bodies to fill the myriad committee roles in the state party structure made it an obvious choice for the Christian Right to work within the Republican Party in the state.

Party laws and traditions have nearly the opposite effect in Indiana, a state with a very similar general ideological profile. While Indiana is, in many ways, just as conservative as Missouri, that underlying concept is expressed differently because the existing power structure in the parties at the advent of the movement was considerably more pragmatic and anti-Christian Right than Missouri's. The movement's focus on legislative politics in Indiana demonstrates the role that broader state law and tradition have on the strategy and fortunes of the Christian Right in state politics.

State law and tradition work to thwart the efforts of the Christian Right in Arizona, however. While the movement has more access and success in Arizona than it does in states where the movement has effectively gone home, this is largely due to its resources, not the political opportunity structure it faces. With a weak party that offers some openings, but ones of seemingly little consequence, the movement has sought to focus its efforts on legislative politics, with only a few victories.

The resources a movement brings to bear on a political situation are important in understanding the degree to which a movement can take advantage of the political opportunity structure in which it is placed. The Christian Right has two significant resources to bring to the political table, numbers and leadership. In Indiana, Missouri, and Arizona, the movement clearly has significant numbers of Evangelicals on which to draw as it tries to impact public policy. In each state, Evangelicals and other conservative religious groups make up at least 25 percent of the population.

The quality and type of leadership that exists in a state also seems to make a significant impact on the strategy and influence of the Christian Right in state-level Republican politics. And it is interesting that the character of the leadership that emerges in a state seems to fit into the pattern of working within and working around in those states. In Missouri, it is very clear that the Christian Right is working within and through the state's Republican Party and all the visible Christian Right leadership in the state has come from within the ranks of the Republican Party. This is not the case in either Indiana or Arizona, where the need to work around the party has necessitated the creation of alternate centers of power generally represented by particular interest groups and their leaders.

Finally, the degree to which the movement can mobilize its constituency based on the level of threat perceived by movement constituents, a form of collective identity production, helps us understand the way the Christian Right and Republican Party interact. There must be some motivation for a movement to organize in the first place, and social movements use societal threat as a way to mobilize support. Thus, in some ways, level of threat is constant. However, there are identifiable differences among the level and kind of threat perceived by the Christian Right in Indiana, Missouri, and Arizona. In Missouri and Arizona, the movement definitely feels threatened, and activists have little trouble mobilizing grassroots support in response to this threat. Indiana presents an entirely different story with a religious conservative constituency that feels relatively unthreatened by state policies, primarily because they tend toward the conservative end of the political spectrum without Christian Right advocacy. This explains why the movement is perceived to have less influence than it might, even in a context where abortion is restricted and gay marriage prohibited.

## FURTHER EVIDENCE FROM OTHER STATES

It is clear that my theory concerning the importance of the interrelationship with the Republican Party for the Christian Right's strategy choices and level of influence in state-level Republican politics helps explain the ways that political opportunity structure, movement resources and threat mobilization impact the movement in Indiana, Missouri, and Arizona. But to demonstrate that this perspective is helpful in understanding the variation we see in Christian Right influence and strategy across all states, the available evidence must be expanded. Because of the diligent work of many other political scientists over the past several decades, such data do exist in the form of a collection of short case studies compiled in the five edited volumes discussed in Chapter 2.[1] These edited volumes contain chapters on the Christian Right in state politics for the 1994, 1996, 1998, 2000, and 2004 election cycles. In all, this represents evidence from an additional twenty states, giving me data from a total of twenty-six states (including the states discussed in Chapter 7).

In each case, it was fairly easy to identify the type of strategy the Christian Right uses in individual states based on the narrative case studies. In some, the authors even pointed out directly the degree to which the movement was involved in party politics or the reasons for its absence from the Republican Party organization. The assignment of strategy type to each state is my own, based on my reading of each state's case studies. I looked for the same information on which to base my rating as I did for the case studies in this book. How is the Christian Right's activity organized? Do they work through the Republican Party or through the legislature? What evidence is there of strategic choices being made? Because the states for these volumes were chosen based on the perception that the movement has influence in the particular state, in every case, the movement had chosen a working within or working around strategy. None had gone home. Thus we need to keep this point in mind when examining the relationship between influence and strategy.

Table 8.1 lists these states and the strategy the movement has chosen in each state, as well as the level of influence the movement is perceived to have in that state.[2] Looking at the strategy column, we see that in a majority of these states, the movement has chosen to work within the Republican Party organization in order to influence state politics and policy. Of the twenty-six states listed, Christian Right uses a working within strategy in fifteen states, it pursues a working around strategy in nine states, and the movement has gone home in two states. Clearly, the movement has taken the opportunity to work within the party as often as it can, and these results reflect the degree to which the movement has assimilated itself into the Republican Party in states all across the country. So, while two of the three case studies in this book offer a picture of working around the party, it seems that in many states—or at least in those states where the movement is perceived to be active and influential— the movement is experiencing significant success within the party. Of course, this sample is somewhat skewed given that these cases were chosen primarily as examples of states where the movement is strong and active. But it does suggest that distinct strategies are being chosen in different states. It is quite evident that the movement has not chosen an overall strategy where deviations are exceptions.

The information available about these states from the existing case studies further demonstrates that the political process model helps us understand the choices the Christian Right has made in how it has sought influence in state politics. It is clear that the political opportunity structures of these states, the resources available to the movement in these states, and the degree to which threat perception is motivating grassroots mobilization has created situations in which the movement has decided to work within or around the Republican Party. A brief examination of some of the specific state contexts demonstrates the point.

The political opportunity structure is clearly encouraging the Christian Right to work within the Republican Party in Iowa and Minnesota. In both of these states, fewer numbers of Evangelicals make it less likely for the movement to be able

**Table 8.1** Christian Right Strategy and Influence by State

| State | Strategy | Level of influence (2004) |
| --- | --- | --- |
| AL | Working within | High |
| AZ | Working around | High |
| CA | Working within | Medium |
| CO | Working within | High |
| FL | Working around | Medium |
| GA | Working within | High |
| IA | Working within | High |
| IL | Working around | Medium |
| IN | Working around | Medium |
| KS | Working within | High |
| MA | Going Home | Medium |
| ME | Working around | Medium |
| MI | Working within | High |
| MN | Working within | High |
| MO | Working within | Medium |
| NC | Working within | High |
| NY | Working around | Low |
| OH | Working around | Medium |
| OK | Working within | High |
| OR | Working around | High |
| SC | Working within | High |
| TX | Working within | High |
| VA | Working within | Medium |
| VT | Going home | Medium |
| WA | Working within | Medium |
| WV | Working around | Medium |

*Source*: Perceived Level of Christian Right Influence for 2004 from Conger, "Moral Values Issues and Political Party Organizations," 2009.

to influence state policy across the board. But the structure of both states' Republican parties, centered on precinct caucuses to choose both presidential candidates and party leadership, allows for significant influence by motivated minorities within the party organization. In both cases, the Christian Right movement has chosen to work within the Republican Party. In the beginning of Chapter 3, I briefly discussed Minnesota's experience with a Christian Right–dominated Republican Party. The movement's power within the state and the party has waxed and waned, but the Christian Right remains a significant player in all Republican Party decision making.

It was early in the Christian Right's history in state politics that the movement emerged as a power in Iowa's Republican Party.[3] In 1988, Pat Robertson beat out President George H. W. Bush in the Republican caucuses. The movement used a classic strategy of trying to get as many supporters as possible to attend the caucuses, filling those meetings with Robertson supporters. That early focus on the caucuses allowed Christian Right activists to gain a foothold in the party and to eventually control many of the state-level leadership positions and policy making bodies.[4] Given the overall shape of politics in Iowa, it is clear that a utilization of the caucus system, with the inherent party openness it provides, has allowed Christian Right activists to have an impact in what is basically a moderate Democratic state.

The political opportunity structure is also clearly impacting the choices of the Christian Right in Ohio and Illinois to work around each state's Republican Party. In Ohio, early efforts by the Christian Right focused on the state's very strong Republican Party. In that venue, movement issues and agendas were combined with other strong coalition members to create compromise positions.[5] The movement had difficulty controlling the situation because the Republican Party already had strong leadership and resources, giving it fewer openings to utilize. So the movement moved to efforts outside the mainstream—and moderate—Republican Party in order to help pass a marriage definition ballot initiative in 2004.

The Illinois Republican Party presents a similar situation to Christian Right activists. It is a strong party with few openings for insurgency, and its focus on economic issues make the core interests of the Christian Right a hard sell within the party. Further, persistent and open corruption in the party have made it clear that an entrenched power base runs the party and that perhaps the party is not as attractive a goal for Christian Right activists as it might be in other states.[6] But the movement has been at work in statewide elections and has raised the profile of religious and moral issues among non-Evangelical groups.

The role of Christian Right movement resources in creating a situation where the movement can work within a state's Republican Party is also clear from many of the state case studies. This is particularly true in southern states, the traditional base of Christian Right strength in the United States. There are significantly more Evangelicals in southern states, and this produces both a greater impact on state public opinion and a wider group from which good leadership can emerge. So, even in states where the laws and traditions that govern party and state politics are not as open to Christian Right influence, the sheer numbers of Evangelicals in the state give the movement a greater ability to impact politics.

We can see this most clearly in Oklahoma. The Christian Right movement is working within the state's Republican Party and helped produce a party platform in 2000 that had the highest amount of Christian Right issue content of any state Republican Party platform.[7] In Oklahoma, the Christian Right has a large number of Evangelicals on which to draw, and quite a number of socially conservative, movement sympathetic party activists.[8] This has translated into power within the party in ways that are almost uncontested. Citizens of Oklahoma largely share the conservative social values of the movement, whether they are Republicans or Democrats, and this overwhelming agreement has created significant opportunities for the movement within the party.

Similarly within the state of Georgia, large numbers of Evangelicals and well-organized and gifted leadership cadre has allowed the Christian Right to work within the state's Republican Party with great success. Unlike Oklahoma, however, the movement has not had an overwhelming effect on state-level policy beyond the party. There is significant enough opposition—particularly in the Democratic African American community in the state—that Republicans have not had the same policy victories in Georgia that they have in other southern states. But, it is clear that the movement has had a significant impact on the Republican Party, both in terms of rank-and-file support and in the quality of the party leadership that has been spawned from within the Christian Right. Most obvious was the role of Ralph Reed as executive director of the state's Republican Party and a candidate for lieutenant governor in 2006. While Reed's star has dimmed because of his involvement in the Jack Abramoff lobbying and money laundering scandal, he was only the most prominent of a large stable of politically gifted movement leaders in Georgia.

As demonstrated in Chapter 7, the lack of movement resources has a significant impact on the Christian Right's ability to compete within the political arena at all. We can see this just as clearly in those states where the movement has some impact, but must work around the Republican Party because of a lack of grassroots support or a closed party system. Maine represents a particularly good example of how the movement can be forced to work around the Republican Party in a situation where it does not have a significant amount of internal resources on which to draw. Maine is about 25 percent Evangelical, but its social conservatism on gay rights is bolstered by a homogenous and conservative population, particularly in the French-Catholic areas of the state's north and west.[9] Yet, the Christian Right has little power in Maine, and very little in the state's Republican Party. Most of the movement's efforts have centered on the Maine Christian Civic League, a political interest group started in 1897 to support the temperance movement. The organization has been successful in keeping Maine's laws unsupportive of gay rights, particularly through the citizen initiative process. Thus we see the Christian Right being entrepreneurial in a political opportunity structure that allows some openings in state politics. The movement may have no chance of policy change within the Republican Party because of the structure of the Republican Party, but it can make the difference in statewide ballot initiatives.

Similarly, the Christian Right significantly hampered by a lack of Evangelicals and the advent of opposition in states like Florida. The movement can draw on considerable resources from Evangelicals in certain parts of Florida, particularly the interior city of Orlando and parts of the western coast. But, the movement has prompted significant opposition statewide because of the large numbers of social liberals in the southern part of the state. This contrast between significant support and opposition based on geography extends to the Republican Party as well. The Christian Right in the Republican Party is what one party activist described as "a necessary annoyance."[10] In this way the internal resources of the movement in Florida place it in an awkward position. It is able to impact politics, but not in the holistic way the movement desires. The Christian Right has worked outside the Republican Party to get sympathetic state legislators elected and has had impact in that arena. However, its lack of influence across the state has limited it to only "medium" influence.[11]

As we saw in the three primary case studies, Christian Right supporters' perception that they are threatened by American culture or politics remains fairly constant throughout the states. Although as we saw in Indiana, a reduced sense of state-level threat may reduce the level of mobilization possible. But as we also saw in Missouri, a heightened perception of threat may motivate supporters of the movement to be more active than the resources and political structures of the state suggest they might be. The evidence from the further case studies suggests that these processes may help increase the level of Christian Right activism in other states as well.

Perhaps the clearest example of the power of threat mobilization to impact the Christian Right's ability to pursue influence in a state's Republican politics is in Oregon. Like Arizona, the movement has sought influence within the Republican Party, but found that working around the party through a variety of outside organizations has led to more significant political influence. As we have seen in a variety of other states, working around the Republican Party option was made viable by the presence of progressive citizen referenda and ballot initiative laws. The Oregon Citizens Alliance (OCA) formed the base from which the Christian Right originally sought to impact the Republican Party and later, after several tries,[12] successfully banned same-sex marriage in Oregon through popular initiative in 2004. This policy success was somewhat of a surprise, given the prevalence of liberal opinions on social issues among voters in the Northwest. Observers suggest that it was this state liber-alness, and the attendant perception of threat it created among Evangelicals and other social conservatives, that allowed OCA and other organizations like it to mobilize to take advantage of a favorable opportunity structure for group action.

Like Indiana, Missouri, and Arizona, the situations in the states observed by other scholars of religion and politics demon-strate how the Christian Right utilizes a state's political oppor-tunity structure, the internal resources of the movement, and the perception of threat leading to grassroots mobilization in order to decide on its strategy of political influence. The infor-mation provided in the case studies of states where the Chris-tian Right has observable influence further demonstrates that the movement will work within or work around the Republican Party depending on the state context in which it finds itself. The fact that these processes are obvious in a wide variety of states demonstrates the usefulness of my theory in explaining the variation in strategy across a wide variety of different state movements and political contexts.

## STRATEGY AND INFLUENCE

This variation in strategy also relates to the variation in influ-ence that is so obvious across the states. Looking back at Table 8.1, we can observe that the level of influence the movement enjoys varies from state to state. This is an ordinal measure of perceived influence based on state level observers' perceptions of the movement's influence in the Republican Party.[13] It is clear that this sample of states includes many where the Chris-tian Right holds substantial influence in the state's Republican Party. Only in New York is the movement's impact perceived to be low. As an ordinal measure, this rating of the Christian Right's influence is necessarily blunt. But the categorical nature of the strategy measure makes influence more appropriately compared when scaled as an ordinal variable.

There exist other measures that give influence a more specific, continuous measure in state Republican politics.[14] In other work, I examine influence more quantitatively and demonstrate the usefulness of the political process model in explaining the variation of influence on its own. As discussed in Chapter 2, I find that influence alone is strongly related to party laws, movement resources, and the availability of ballot initiatives and referenda. The previous research, however, stops at explaining influence variation and does not allow me to explain Christian Right strategy as the analyses in this book do. So based on earlier work on influence and the examination of a variety of data in this book, we can now link political opportunity structure, movement resources, and threat mobilization to Christian Right influence and strategy in the states individually. But if the underlying concepts of PPM are having an impact on both the influence and strategy of a movement, how might it impact the two together to create the political situation we can observe in each state?

One way to examine this is to look at the way strategy and influence are related to one another in each state. Returning to Table 8.1, it is quickly apparent that movement strategy does not directly predict movement influence. While it is clear from the qualitative case study data, both my own and other scholars', that the political opportunity structure, movement resources, and threat mobilization affect both strategy and success, it is also clear that there is not a monotonic relationship between the two. For example, the Christian Right in Arizona has had more (though limited) success in the state's Republican Party organization than has the movement in Indiana, but that has not translated into more influence over state policy. The movement has had more successes in Indiana. But as the movement adapts itself to its political environment, it will seek what policy influence it can, be that through the party or around it.

However, the relationship between strategy and influence described in Table 8.1 does suggest that there is some sort of connection between the two, based on the constraints under which the Christian Right works. Table 8.2 shows the crosstabs and attendant measures of association for movement strategy and influence. The data demonstrate that for states with a high level of perceived influence, the movement is much more likely to choose a strategy that allows it to work within the party. Of the thirteen high influence states, only two seem to be exhibiting a working around strategy. There is only one state in my sample where the Christian Right seems to be exhibiting low influence, and in that state the movement is trying to work around the party. The states in the medium influence category, however, are much more evenly distributed across strategy choices. In the majority of states, the movement seems to be working around the party, while in a large minority, it is working around.[15]

Interestingly, this relationship also holds up when submitted to statistical testing. For the twenty-six states included in this analysis, the relationship between strategy and influence approaches traditional levels of statistical significance ( $x^2$, $p$ = 0.084). And while the degree of association as measured by Lambda ($\lambda$) is small (0.118), it is also statistically significant ($p$ = 0.049). Thus it does seem that there is some relationship between the type of strategy chosen by the Christian Right and the movement's influence in a particular state. Perceived

**Table 8.2** Crosstabs and Association between Movement Strategy and Influence

| Strategy/ influence | High | Medium | Low | Total |
|---|---|---|---|---|
| Working within | 11 | 4 | 0 | 15 |
| Working around | 2 | 6 | 1 | 9 |
| Going home | 0 | 2 | 0 | 2 |
| Total | 13 | 12 | 1 | 26 |

*Source*: Perceived Level of Christian Right Influence for 2004 from Conger, "Moral Values Issues and Political Party Organizations," 2009.

$\lambda$ = .118 (.055), $p$ = 0.049

$x^2$ = 11.133, $p$ = 0.084

influence seems to be linked to working within the party. But because I am not able to test these relationships in a fully quantitative way due to lack of strategy data from all fifty states, I can only speculate that more data would demonstrate a stronger relationship. I rely on my theory to suggest that the movement's influence is not caused by their strategy, at least in a straightforward way, but that the underlying context faced by the movement is the true predictor of both strategy and influence.

These results further strengthen my larger conclusions as well. Because strategy and influence seem to be related to one another, this suggests that Christian Right activists all over the country are going through the process of looking for the best way to influence state politics and policy and coming to similar conclusions within each state. The fact that many successful state movements are working within the Republican Party further bolsters my assertion that the movement starts with the party first because it offers the most benefits. Both influence and strategy are shaped by the context in which the movement is operating and the relationship between the two demonstrates that they are appropriate linked—and studied—together.

Again, we must be cautious about these results because of the nature of the states from which this sample is drawn. However, we can have a reasonable amount of confidence in them because the sample is skewed toward those states where Christian Right influence is more than a negligible factor in state politics. My theory assumes that those states in which the movement has gone home, it has little influence. Therefore I do seem to be capturing the nature of the relationship between strategy and influence for those states where influence is greater, and the lack of other states does not present a problem for results on the higher end of the influence spectrum.

In this chapter, I have sought to elaborate more fully on the relationship between strategy choice and level of movement influence and to link together the evidence from the case studies to help us better understand how the Christian Right chooses to interact with the Republican Party in each state. Following the insights of the PPM, we can now see how the political opportunity structure, the resources available to the

Christian Right, and its ability to mobilize constituents based on perception of threat help us to understand in a more comprehensive way the choices a movement makes as it seeks to influence state politics and policy, and the ways in which this context constrains not only the Christian Right's relationship with the Republican Party, but also the degree to which the movement is able to achieve its policy goals. Most important, I have taken these insights a step further and sought to understand how strategy and influence are related to one another. It seems likely that underlying constraints affect the movement's strategic choices—as we saw in the case studies—but influence is affected both by these underlying constraint and the strategy choices made by the movement. This complex relationship is best explored qualitatively, but even the basic quantitative analysis that is possible seems to confirm my theoretical understanding of the situation. Overall, it seems that a wide range of evidence confirms the idea that the Christian Right, when faced with a state's Republican Party organization, chooses to work within it, work around it, or to go home, based on the political opportunity structure it faces, its internal resources, and the level of threat perceived by its supporters.

# CHAPTER 9

———————❦———————

# CONCLUSION

## THE CHRISTIAN RIGHT AND THE CONTEXT
## OF REPUBLICAN STATE POLITICS

More than perhaps any other contemporary social movement, the Christian Right is ingrained in the fabric of American state politics. Its influence is felt in nearly every state and its impact is clear in the Republican Party and in public policy decision making. Christian Right supporters form the backbone of the activist and volunteer cadre in the Republican Party and have rebuilt local parties in many areas. Movement supporters have been elected to all levels of state and local government—from school boards to the state legislature—and many activists have become lobbyists who use their expertise to influence a wide variety of political issues and policies. Thus Christian Right activists are clearly well integrated into state politics and they are exerting influence on public policy at all levels.

This demonstrates the unique position of the Christian Right in American politics. As one of the few observable social movement on the right, religious conservatives and the Christian Right make up between 30 percent and 40 percent of Republican voters in any given state. These numbers give the movement much of its inherent political clout and give movement leaders' arguments for the support of their issue positions real weight in political discourse. America is, on the whole, a highly religious country where more than 80 percent of the general population believes in God. Unlike its Western European counterparts, religious adherence in the United States has remained high through the last century of modernization and economic growth. During many periods in American history, religious conviction has been the catalyst for social movements that sought to change public policy to coincide with a particular set of moral views. The abolitionists and the temperance movement are only the two most obvious examples of this impulse from American history. Christian Right supporters and activists are the heirs to these religious believers who have been active in American politics on both sides of the aisle. In this way, we can see how the unique characteristics of American religion, including large numbers of Evangelical Christians, have contributed to a situation where the Christian Right has a near monopoly on social movement activity on the right side of the political spectrum in the United States. The Christian Right has been the only movement with the wherewithal to take advantage of the openings provided by the structure of Republican politics and the only movement conservative enough in its aims to be a good candidate for right-leaning political activism. Further, the movement has succeeded in changing policy and politics in tangible ways. In many states the movement has succeeded in significantly limiting abortion license and defining marriage as a union between one man and one woman, and the political rhetoric required of most political candidates now includes explicit references to God, the candidates' religious beliefs, and how these will impact a person's decisions once in office.

For these reasons, it is clear that the Christian Right movement matters in contemporary American politics. It also matters because of the things it teaches us about politics in the United States. The movement's interaction with Republican politics shows us how social movements evolve and are integrated into the political systems in which they seek change. This links the conclusions of this book into the larger theoretical conversations taking place in political science and sociology about the life cycles and success of social movements. Further, and perhaps more important, the interactions between the Christian Right and state Republican politics teaches us about the ways in which political context, internal resources, and mobilization processes constrain the behavior and strategy of a movement seeking power in state politics. Politics is a dynamic process, one that requires scholars to be keenly aware of context, even as we seek to identify and explain political phenomena.

One of the best ways to capture this dynamic process is to combine both quantitative and qualitative research as I have in this book. The qualitative portion of this project—the case studies on Indiana, Missouri, Arizona, and states where the movement has gone home—shows not only how the Christian Right and Republican Party interact in these states, but also allows us to understand *when* and *how* the movement matters to state Republican politics. These cases provide the details that allow us to fully understand the dynamics of the political process in an individual state. Other quantitative research and the exploration of the relationship between strategy and influence in Chapter 8 demonstrate that the movement matters all over the country and that the success of the movement is inextricably linked to the constraints the Christian Right faces. Thus we can see both how strategy and influence of the Christian Right are shaped by the political context in which it operates.

In this book, I have sought to provide a theoretical explanation for how the Christian Right pursues influence on policy making at the state level and the movement's success in impacting Republican and state politics. When the Christian Right— or any social movement—approaches a political system, it has three choices: the movement can seek power within the political party, it can work around it, or it can eschew politics altogether. The strategy chosen by a Christian Right movement in a particular state is based upon the political opportunity structure in which the movement finds itself, its internal resources and the degree to which constituents can be mobilized by perceptions of threat. While this theory was developed in relation to the Christian Right and state Republican parties in the United States, there is no reason to think that these tenets should not hold in other political and social contexts. While overlapping, the pro-life movement in the United States is not synonymous with the Christian Right. Its focus on state-level activity makes it another good example of how a movement has adapted its strategy to a state's political context. And further, the Libertarian movement in the western United States, which has worked both through and around Republican state parties, is another example of a movement that should fit within the explanations provided by my theory.

We can see social movements taking advantage of the openings provided by the structure of state politics on the left in the United States as well. Since at least the 1960s, modern social movements have been a fundamental part of the Democratic Party. We can look farther back in history to see a similar situation during the Progressive Era. But the Democratic Party has become almost defined by the movements it has encompassed in the last forty years. Feminists, African Americans, gays and lesbians, and environmentalists all represent social movement activists who have become integral parts of the Democratic Party. Democrats have tended to have party rules that favor citizen involvement to a greater degree than have Republicans. Since the reforms of the 1970s, many parts and functions of the party are reserved specifically for group representation. These factors have greatly contributed to the ability of social movements to seek public policy influence through the Democratic Party. Thus my theory should help explain the relationship among social movements and the Democratic Party as well. Perhaps the best example would be the gay and lesbian movement in the Democratic Party. It has focused on state-level politics, its strategy, and success seem to vary across the states based on the criteria laid down by the theory.

The story of the Christian Right and the Republican Party remains somewhat novel simply because other groups have not yet challenged the supremacy of the Christian Right on the right. While it is certainly possible to explain why this has been the case up to this point, there is no reason to think that contemporary politics precludes the advent of another strong social movement on the right. A generation from now, Republicans may find themselves to be just as much of a party representing distinct groups with overlapping interests as the Democrats are today.

This theory is an important step forward in our understanding of not only the Christian Right, but also of how social movements, in general, interact with political parties and how the context of social movement activities affects the nature and character of a movement and its success. Building on a wealth of empirical data collected over the life of the Christian Right, I believe this theory most clearly accounts for the way we see the movement behaving in contemporary politics and the level of success the movement has achieved in a variety of states.

The evidence offered in the previous chapters supports this theory and demonstrates how it works on a practical level in state politics. As particularly demonstrated in the state case studies, Indiana, Missouri, and Arizona, we can see how the Christian Right definitely makes strategic choices to work within the Republican Party, to work around it, or to go home. Further, these decisions and the success with which they meet are demonstrably based on the political opportunity structure, movement resources, and threat mobilization in the state. In each state, it is readily apparent that the strategic choices of the Christian Right are directly linked to the context in which it finds itself. Party rules, state law, legislative process, ballot and referenda abilities, the leadership and extent of the Christian Right, and perceptions of threat all define the constraints the movement faces and determine the course of action it pursues. This is further demonstrated by the lack of Christian Right influence exhibited in those states where the movement's best strategy has been to go home, and not participate in the political process.

## State Context and Strategic Choice

In the end, there are three main points we can draw from this analysis. First, state context matters. In some ways this finding seems obvious; of course the movement would appear and act differently in different states. V. O. Key[1] was the first to point out the importance of the differences between the states, but little of the religion and politics literature has taken this into account. There are fifty state political systems, fifty state Republican parties, and fifty Christian Right movements. The notion that context, particularly the state political structure that surrounds the movement, has a determinative role in the ability of the Christian Right to influence politics is a new finding. This allows us to look at each state as its own entity, taking account of its unique characteristics, but also to understand the dynamics of the movement as a whole and to make generalizations that help us understand the underlying phenomenon. Although each state's context differs, we can identify regularities that help predict what type of characteristics and success the movement will have in each state.

The regularities within each state's context can be thought of generically as the state's political opportunity structure. The state's laws, the rules that govern the Republican Party's organization and leadership choices, and the ways in which the legislative and executive branches do business all have a great impact on the Christian Right's ability to influence state public policy. As we have seen throughout our exploration of how the Christian Right works within or around the Republican Party in a state, these political opportunity structures matter for a number of reasons. The structure of a state's politics, how policy is made and the business of politics is accomplished, is important to the strategy pursued by the movement. The Christian Right behaves rationally within these structures; it seeks to achieve the greatest influence it can within the constraints with which it is faced. Thus what the structure actually looks like—how an idea becomes public policy in a state—has tremendous impact on the strategic choices of the movement and its supporters.

Political opportunity structure matters to the individual activist as well. As an individual learns how to negotiate a state's political system, how to influence public policy in desired ways, that person becomes more politically sophisticated. In fact it was the personal conversations with activists that originally alerted me to the underlying story of how the movement operates. In each state where I talked with Christian Right activists, they told me detailed stories of how particular policy victories—or defeats—had taken place. These stories were replete with intricate details, including how the Republican Party organization in each state operates and makes decisions, how bills are considered within the state legislatures and most strikingly, the network of political relationships that each activist maintained in order to see their policy positions prevail. Many, in fact, told stories about how they originally came by this knowledge; usually involving significant work on their part to learn the processes and personalities of the state's Republican Party and larger government environment. So the political opportunity structure is important to individual activists because it is their growing knowledge of their state's political context and the ability to work within it that demonstrates their learning and evolution in politics.[2] I believe this accounts for the large overlap between Christian Right and Republican grassroots activists in many states. Activists needed to learn how to use the system to get what they want and were able to leverage that knowledge into positions of power within the party and even in the larger state government. This political sophistication provides even more evidence for my theory. Christian Right activists have individually been rational actors and have concentrated on the areas in each state where their activity will have the most impact.

The demonstration that the movement is responding to the political opportunity structure in which it operates—a state's context—fills a significant gap in our understanding of how religion and politics operates in the United States. Religiously based political movements like the Christian Right have generally been approached as if the religious dimension of their activity was the primary factor in determining their operation and success. But this book demonstrates that, in fact, the Christian Right is constrained like all other social movements by the context in which it operates. The religious beliefs of its supporters and activists may provide a unique glue to hold the movement together and an important resource for mobilization. However, it is clear that those religious beliefs are still filtered through political context as they try to impact state policy and politics.

The second main point we can draw from the analyses in this project is that the movement itself, its resources and internal strength, matters. This finding supports much of the previous research on the Christian Right and its place in American state politics, but it also supports the larger conclusions of this book, namely that movement resources are definitive *in conjunction* with the political context faced by the party. The Christian Right is able to exert the power that it has because of the internal resources it can bring to bear on the political realm. Because it is a social movement, the Christian Right is very dependent not only on the number of religious conservatives and Evangelicals in a state, but also the network that is formed within these populations. Religion provides not only the impetus for political action and the social capital necessary for successful participation, but is also a distinctive connection that ties Christian Right activists and supporters together in ways that may be unique among social movements. We have seen that the movement thrives in some states where there are no identifiable Christian Right groups or even leaders and this is based on the strength of these nonpolitical networks. This is not to say that leadership is unimportant. It is clear from the case studies that good leadership, whether within the Republican Party or outside of it, is paramount to the movement's ability to take advantage of the openings in the political system in which it operates.

Beyond these sorts of organizational resources, the internal character of the movement in each state matters because it must recognize and utilize the threat that religious conservatives feel from the society around them. State movements that feel more threatened are more likely to be successful in exerting influence in Republican politics, even in the face of structural or other movement obstacles. And in states with large Evangelical populations, like Indiana, a lack of a sense of threat limits even skilled movement leadership in what they can accomplish in state politics.

Perhaps the most striking finding of this project has been the way in which the political opportunity structure and resources interact in the context of a state's politics to impact the way the Christian Right is organized in a state. In states where the movement has had significant success in influencing politics and policy through the Republican Party, the movement is generally centered on the party with few identifiable Christian Right organizations. In these states, the movement does not need to have a singular entity such as an interest group coordinating activities. The party itself plays this function, linking supporters and activists together through party activities. In these states, the movement and the party become synonymous to the point that observers tend not to register the movement's influence.

The movement is the party and vice versa. While some activists still choose to work outside the party, they are more likely to be radical and antisystem in their orientation than in other states.

Conversely, in states where the Christian Right has had little success in influencing policy or politics through the Republican Party, it needs a focal point for strategy and activity. Generally, this is an interest group or policy institute whose focus is on the state legislature or ballot initiatives. In these states, the movement tends to be more clearly defined as supporters of the organization. It can also be the case that in states like this, where the movement is not prominent within the party, that the Christian Right may have power within certain geographic areas, focusing activists on the campaigns and activities of particular members of the state legislature or U.S. Congress.

These differences in movement organization based on the context of state politics may further solve the analytic problem of why observers do not register strong influence by the Christian Right in Republican parties in the South—the movement's early role in rebuilding local parties notwithstanding. If the movement has great success in the party in these states, as national-level studies demonstrate, then it may be difficult to separate the movement from the party. Based on this theory, and general understandings of the movement in the South, it seems that this may prove to be the best explanation.

Finally, this book demonstrates the important role of strategic choice in understanding how social movements and groups pursue political goals in American politics. Every movement makes choices about how it will seek to change politics and society. The key finding of these analyses is that those strategic choices are constrained both by the resources and threat mobilization a movement has at its disposal and the political opportunity structure it faces. Strategic choices are not made in a vacuum; they are made in the context of all these considerations. Most activists seem to be making similar choices in each state and it is because they are faced with a similar set of constraints. The movement and the context matter, because without them, there is no basis for the political decisions that we can observe the movement making.

This is an even more important finding when we take a step back and look at the Christian Right movement as a whole, across the entire country. The resources and contexts that serve the movement so well on the state level are, in many ways, not in existence at the national level. There has been no real national leadership to the movement since the heyday of the Christian Coalition in the mid 1990s. And the context of American politics makes it difficult for the movement work around the Republican Party at the national level. While the national party has been open to the movement's influence, it is much more a creature of large donors than are state-level parties. The Christian Right has few of these kinds of donors to help shape the opinions and priorities of the national party. Even in the George W. Bush administration, many national Christian Right activists felt like the strategists and policy consultants around the president were more interested in using the movement's sway with its supporters than in listening to its policy desires. So, the Christian Right has found a much more attractive home in state Republican politics over time because the context of those politics is more suited to the movement's strengths.

This reality may be even more important to the movement as the country transitions to a Democratic administration that appears to be demonstrably less amenable to its policy positions than was the George W. Bush administration. Chaos within the national Republican Party, and an Obama White House and Democratic Congress, make it that much more difficult for Christian Right opinions to be heard at the national level. So, for the foreseeable future, the movement will have its most observable impact in Republican state politics, and it is ready and able to operate successfully within that sphere.

## IMPLICATIONS

Approaching the Christian Right in this way—by examining the context and resources that constraint it—is somewhat of a departure from previous studies of the Christian Right. More unique however, is my focus on the nature and importance of strategic choice in the operations and success of the movement. If my analyses are correct, there are several things we should be able to observe as we look at the Christian Right in the future. First and foremost, we should see the movement continuing to pursue political power in the state arena. The movement has found a home at the state level and is likely to continue to pursue its policy goals in the smaller venues of state and local politics. This is partially because it has been successful there, but also because many of the issues on which the movement concentrates find their most nature expression at the state level. The Christian Right will seek influence where it can achieve that influence. And state-level politics are attractively structured for grassroots and social movement success.

Second, we should be able to observe evolution over time in the tactics and strategies of the Christian Right. These changes occur for two reasons, growing sophistication of Christian Right activists and their ability to utilize the resources on hand and structural change within the system. As we have seen in earlier chapters, over time movement activists grow in their political sophistication and their ability to navigate a state's political system. They gain information, knowledge, and experience that allow them to more effectively press their issue positions both within and outside of the Republican Party. This sophistication is not to the benefit of the individual activists alone, however. Much of it is passed on to subsequent waves of activists, producing a situation where the entire movement is gaining sophistication and experience from individuals' activism. Thus, as the movement and its supporters learn the rules of the game, the structures that constrain their activities and success, they will over time show an increasing ability to be successful as they learn how best to pursue their goals.

We should also be able to observe distinct changes in behavior based on changes in a state's political context—whether great or small. The crux of my argument is that the Christian Right is responding to its environment with the resources it can bring to bear, working within political constraints to achieve its goals. Therefore we should see the movement adjust itself to a dynamic political environment by taking advantage of changes in state campaign finance laws or court rulings that make ballot initiatives or referenda easier to pursue. So when laws, customs, or the personalities in power change, we should see the movement alter its strategy—and its expectations for success—accordingly.

Finally, if my analysis of Christian Right politics at the state level is correct, we should be able to observe similar links between political context and the strategies and characteristics of the Christian Right movement in every state, not just the ones studied for this project. Although my focus in this book is primarily on Indiana, Missouri, and Arizona, I have offered evidence from other states as well, demonstrating that this theoretical understanding of the movement should work across the country. Thus, while in-depth observations of other states will lend more nuance and generalizability to my analytic approach, I believe the general focus on the political process model will continue to provide a useful framework for examining the Christian Right or other social movements engaged in seeking influence over public policy making in a partisan-driven system.

My analysis and interpretation of the data brings up another ancillary, but important question. If the context of state politics impacts the ability of social movements to influence political parties and state politics, and if the space for the Christian Right in Republican politics is so clearly evident in many states, why have other social movements not taken advantage of these beneficial conditions as well? I believe that the potential for this kind of development certainly exists; political opportunity structure, movement resources, and threat mobilizations have provided ample opportunity for other political insurgencies, but the unique political and social situation of the American right has made it unclear whether other social movements will, in fact, arise and follow the Christian Right's path.

Using the context of state politics as the explanation for Christian Right political strategies has implications for our understanding of the future shape and importance of the movement in American politics. If my analysis is correct, then how we examine social movements and their ability to impact public policy should be seen through the lens of both the internal and external constraints under which they operate. We should be able to eventually observe changes in the Christian Right linked to changes in state context and may eventually see other right-leaning social movements challenge the dominance of the Christian Right in Republican politics.

## WHAT COMES NEXT?

First and foremost, it makes sense to closely observe other states at the in-depth case study level to see if the context of state politics explains Christian Right strategy as well as it does in Indiana, Missouri, and Arizona. I believe that the theory will continue to provide insights across the states, particularly in those states where the movement has some, but not overwhelming impact. My theory helps to elucidate the strategic choices movement activists must make, and these choices are more clearly on display in those states where the Christian Right exists in an environment somewhere between total success and total failure.

Related to this, it seems that more work is necessary to fully flesh out the implications of the theory in regards to states where the movement has effectively gone home. In these states there are generally few Evangelicals and the movement exhibits little influence in state politics and little activity to achieve any influence. Because of the historical lack of scholarly focus on such states in regard to the Christian Right movement, more research needs to be done to understand where the threshold of movement resources lies, and how religious conservatives behave in states with numbers below that threshold. This may give the theory a better distinction between necessary and sufficient causation for Christian Right influence. Both a level of support above the threshold minimum and an open political structure seem to be necessary for the Christian Right to choose a Republican Party strategy, but neither appears sufficient from our current perspective. Further research should flesh this out and provide a clearer picture of how state political context and movement resources work together to provide the Christian Right with the openings it needs to be influential in state Republican politics.

Finally, this explanation of how the Christian Right operates within state politics provides a picture of the larger realm of social movements interacting with political institutions, particularly political parties. Therefore more research is needed to determine how well this theory explains social movement situations beyond the Christian Right movement in the United States. Perhaps future work could apply the theory to the gay and lesbian movement within Democratic state politics or even the European pro-life movement. While I am confident that this approach will be fruitful in helping us gain a more comprehensive view of how social movements fit into every-day, nonrevolutionary politics, confirmation of its claims will be advanced by further and wider-ranging study. It is my hope that with more examples and a richer body of data on which to draw, the theory can be refined and expanded to be useful for middle-class social movements in a variety of different contexts.

The Christian Right plays an enormous role in contempo-rary American politics. This is particularly true in Republican politics and at the state level. The advent of the movement has signaled a sea change in American politics in a number of ways. First, Evangelicals and fundamentalists, having removed themselves from politics for most of the twentieth century, have returned to the arena with vigor and passion and a focus on changing public policy. Second, the Christian Right is the first modern social movement to emerge in the United States on the right side of the political spectrum. The growing affluence and educational attainment of Evangelicals have driven this phe-nomenon and provide the basis for the engaged and sophisti-cated Christian Right activists we can observe in contemporary American politics. Most importantly for the everyday lives of American citizens, the movement has concentrated its efforts over the last decade on the arena of state politics, and more specifically on state Republican parties.

The Christian Right is fascinating to study for this very rea-son; it can give us insight into the inner workings of an impor-tant political player in contemporary politics. But more than that, the movement gives us a window onto state politics as it is experienced by those citizens and activists who desire political participation beyond voting. It helps us to understand policy making at a basic and important level, the interplay of influ-ences and agendas that go into the processes that eventually produce and enforce these policies. Thus understanding the Christian Right movement in its state-level incarnation gives us a more comprehensive picture of politics and political processes in the United States.

At a higher level, though, the Christian Right and its attempts to influence public policy at the state level give us insight into the larger questions of how social movements operate, make strategy, and interact with the political context around them. The Christian Right serves as an exemplar of an organized and motivated movement and helps us to see why movements succeed—or fail—in changing society through political means. For this reason we can link the insights gained in observing the Christian Right to a more general understanding of social movements, political institutions, and political processes. This gives the movement a life beyond itself and provides us with the ingredients of a much richer and more nuanced understanding of real politics, as it actually happens, for millions of citizens in democratic countries around the world.

# APPENDIX

---✦---

# INTERVIEW PROTOCOL

1. "Tell me about your involvement in _____."
2. "Tell me about the Republican party in your state."

   a. Probe for:
      i. Strength (staff, money, and SERVICE relative to similar states?)
      ii. Structure and permeability
      iii. How is the leadership chosen?
      iv. State-Level activities (candidate support, issue agendas, etc.)
      v. Who makes decisions? How are they communicated? (state committee, county chairs legislative leadership, governor, etc.)
      vi. Are there factions, coalitions within the party?

3. "Tell me about the activity of religious conservatives in your state."

   a. Probe for:
      i. First emergence and Historical level of influence
      ii. Specific or "turning point" events
      iii. Important issues/groups/leaders
      iv. How are people mobilized? Groups or grassroots?
      v. Internal cohesion among groups
      vi. General level of influence (current)
      vii. Public Opinion of CR/"fellow travelers."
      viii. Ties to larger Evangelical community/friend networks, Christian organizations.
      ix. Perception of threat from policy, state or national

4. "What has the relationship between Religious Conservatives and the Republican Party been like in your state?"

    a. Probe for:
        i. General opinion of the party about the movement and vice versa
        ii. Central Issues
        iii. RC Tactics and success – "What do they do? Are they good at it?"
        iv. State committee presence
        v. Candidate Nominations/State Legislative Agenda
        vi. Conflict within party? Accommodations? On either side?
        vii. Has their presence changed the party? The RC Activists? Assimilation?

5. "What do I need to know to really understand the politics of your state?"
6. "What issues are on the horizon that you think important for the RP/RC relationship?"
7. "Am I missing anything? Who else should I be talking to?"

# NOTES

## CHAPTER 1

1. May, "Robertson Exhorts Followers," 14.
2. D'Antonio, "Bedeviling the GOP," 28.
3. Diamond, *Not by Politics Alone*; della Porta and Diani, *Social Movements*; Kriesi et al., *New Social Movements in Western Europe*; Tarrow, *Power in Movement*.
4. Reed, *Politically Incorrect*; Watson, *The Christian Coalition*.
5. Diamond, *Not by Politics Alone*, 11.
6. Moen, *The Transformation of the Christian Right*.
7. George and Bennet, *Case Studies and Theory Development*.
8. Conger and Green, "Spreading Out and Digging In"; Persinos, "Has the Christian Right Taken Over the Republican Party?"
9. Green, Rozell, and Wilcox, *Marching to the Millennium*; Rozell and Wilcox, *God at the Grassroots*; Rozell and Wilcox, *God at the Grassroots 1996*.
10. Fenno, *HomeStyle*.
11. Hertzke, *Echoes of Discontent*; Rozell and Wilcox, *Second Coming*.
12. George and Bennet, *Case Studies and Theory Development*, 176; Tansey, "Process-Tracing and Elite Interviewing."

## CHAPTER 2

1. In the last years of the nineteenth century, the free silver movement sought to move the United States away from the gold standard in currency and to use silver coins as well. This would have caused significant inflation and would have allowed farmers, laborers, and other working-class people to pay their debts with cheaper money, thus taking some power away from banks, businesses, and wealthy people. Bryan's defeat in the presidential elections of 1896, 1900, and 1908 ensured that the movement never achieved its goals.
2. Lienesch, *In the Beginning*.

3. The links between the New Right and the Christian Right were strong enough that many early commentators talked of the "New Christian Right." While there certainly was overlap, these are distinct movements with New Right philosophy being most clearly expressed in contemporary American politics by the concerns of Neoconservatives and their focus on American foreign policy.

4. Guth, "The Politics of the Christian Right."

5. Cromartie, "Religious Conservatives In American Politics 1980–2000."

6. Edsall and Von Drehle, "Life in the Grand Old Party," A1.

7. Reichley, *The Life of the Parties*, 375.

8. Klandermans, Kriesi, and Tarrow, *From Structure to Action*; Kriesi et al., *New Social Movements in Western Europe*.

9. Tarrow, *Power in Movement*.

10. Oldfield, *The Right and the Righteous*, 101.

11. Guth, "The Politics of the Christian Right?" 36.

12. Wilcox, *Onward Christian Soldiers?*

13. Blumenthal, "Christian Soldiers."

14. Moen, *The Transformation of the Christian Right*, 113.

15. Diamond, *Not by Politics Alone*, 76.

16. Moen, *The Transformation of the Christian Right*, 117.

17. Diamond, *Not by Politics Alone*, 79.

18. Corrado, "The Politics of Cohesion," 77.

19. Ibid., 78.

20. Mydans, "Christian Conservatives Counting Hundreds of Gains in Local Votes."

21. Rozell and Wilcox, *God at the Grassroots*, 255–56.

22. Diamond, *Not by Politics Alone*; Guth, "The Politics of the Christian Right"; Moen, *The Transformation of the Christian Right*.

23. Reed, *Politically Incorrect*; Reed, *Active Faith*.

24. Thomas and Dobson, *Blinded by Might*.

25. Persinos, "Has the Christian Right Taken Over the Republican Party?" 22.

26. Green, Rozell, and Wilcox, *Prayers in the Precincts*.

27. Cooperman, "Churchgoers Get Direction from Bush Campaign," A6.

28. Green, Rozell, and Wilcox, *The Values Campaign?*

29. Smith, "Do the Democrats Have a God Problem?"

30. Faith in Public Life.org, The Young and the Faithful, http://www.faithinpubliclife.org/tools/polls/faps/The%20Young%20and%20the%20Faithful.pdf; Pew Forum on Religion and Public Life, "A

Post-Election Look at Religious Voters in the 2008 Election," http://www.pewforum.org/events/?EventID=209.

31. Herman, "GOP Politics: A Religious Experience."

32. Verba, Schlozman, and Brady, *Voice and Equality.*

33. Bruce, *The Rise and Fall of the New Christian Right*; Capps, *The New Religious Right*; Jorstad, *The New Christian Right 1981–1988*; Martin, *With God on Our Side*; Wilcox, *God's Warrior*; Wilcox, *Onward Christian Soldiers?*

34. Wilson, *Political Organizations.*

35. Cromartie, *No Longer Exiles*; Cromartie, *Disciples and Democracy*; Jelen, "Citizenship, Discipleship, and Democracy"; Lienesch, *Redeeming America*; Moen, "The Evolving Politics of the Christian Right"; Neuhaus and Cromartie, *Piety and Policy*; Smith, *Christian America?*

36. Diamond, *Not by Politics Alone*; Djupe and Neiheisel, "Christian Right Horticulture"; Hertzke, *Echoes of Discontent.*

37. Green, Guth, and Hill, "Faith and Election"; Hertzke, *Representing God in Washington*; Hofrenning, *In Washington But Not of It*; Moen, *The Transformation of the Christian Right.*

38. Wald and Corey, "The Christian Right and Public Policy."

39. Deckman, *School Board Battles.*

40. Bendyna and Wilcox, "The Christian Right Old and New"; Watson, *The Christian Coalition.*

41. Bruce, Kivisto, and Swatos, *The Rapture of Politics*; Green, Rozell, and Wilcox, *Prayers in the Precincts*; Liebman and Wuthnow, *The New Christian Right*; Rozell and Wilcox, *God at the Grassroots*; Smidt and Penning, *Sojourners in the Wilderness*; Urofsky and May, *The New Christian Right.*

42. Green, Rozell, and Wilcox, *Prayers in the Precincts;* Green, Rozell, and Wilcox, *Marching to the Millennium*; Green, Rozell, and Wilcox, *The Values Campaign?*; Rozell and Wilcox, *God at the Grassroots*; Rozell and Wilcox, *God at the Grassroots, 1996.*

43. Blumenthal, "Christian Soldiers."

44. Green and Guth, "The Christian Right in the Republican Party."

45. Green, Guth, and Wilcox, "Less Than Conquerors"; Oldfield, *The Right and the Righteous.*

46. Conger and Green, "Spreading Out and Digging In"; Conger, "A Matter of Context."

47. Green, Guth, and Wilcox, "Less Than Conquerors," 118.

48. Conger, "A Matter of Context."

49. Eldersveld, *Political Parties in American Society;* Rossiter, *Parties and Politics in America;* Schlesinger, *Political Parties and the Winning of Office.*

50. Monroe, *The Political Party Matrix.*

51. Eldersveld and Walton, *Political Parties in American Society,* 10.

52. Gimpel, *National Elections and the Autonomy of American State Party Systems;* Jewell and Morehouse, *Political Parties and Elections in American States;* Jewell and Olson, *Political Parties and Elections in American States.*

53. Weber and Brace, *American State and Local Politics,* 201.

54. Goldstone, *States, Parties, and Social Movements,* 4.

55. della Porta and Rucht, "Social Movement Sectors in Context"; Kriei et al., *New Social Movements in Western Europe;* Kubik, "Institutionalization of Protest"; Maguire, "Opposition Movements and Opposition Parties."

56. Amenta, *Bold Relief;* Cloward and Piven, "Disruptive Dissensus"; Piven and Cloward, *Poor People's Movements.*

57. Baer and Bositis, *Elite Cadres and Party Coalitions.*

58. Goldstone, "Bridging Institutionalized and Noninstitutionalized Politics."

59. Ibid., 24.

60. Dalton, "Strategies of Partisan Influence"; Rucht, "The Strategies and Action Repertoires."

61. Baer and Bositis, *Elite Cadres and Party Coalitions.*

62. Gusfield, *Protest, Reform and Revolt,* 2.

63. Baer and Bositis, *Elite Cadres and Party Coalitions,* 54.

64. della Porta and Diani, *Social Movements,* 121.

65. Ibid., 140.

66. Baer and Bositis, *Elite Cadres and Party Coalitions,* 106.

67. McAdam, *Political Process.*

68. Tarrow, "Paradigm Warriors."

69. Engel, *The Unfinished Revolution;* McAdam, McCarthy, and Zald, "Introduction: Opportunities, Mobilizing Structures, and Framing Processes."

70. Meyer, "Tending the Vineyard," 82.

71. Tarrow, *Power in Movement.*

72. Ansolabeher and King, "Measuring the Consequences"; Carsey et al., "State Party Context and Norms"; Cavala, "Changing the Rules is Changing the Game"; Usher, "Strategy, Rules, and Participation"; and more generally, Engstrom and Kernell, "Manufactured Responsiveness"; North, "Economic Performance Through Time."

73. Engel, *The Unfinished Revolution*; Kitschelt, "Political Opportunity Structure and Political Protest."
74. Kitschelt, "Political Opportunity Structure and Political Protest"; Kriesi et al., *New Social Movements in Western Europe*; Tarrow, "Social Movements in Contentious Politics."
75. Green, Guth, and Wilcox, "Less than Conquerors"; Green, Rozell, and Wilcox, "Social Movements and Party Politics"; Bates, "The Decline of a New Christian Right Social Movement Organization."
76. Wald, Silverman, and Fridy, "Making Sense of Religion."
77. Green, Guth, and Wilcox, "Less than Conquerors"; Green, Rozell, and Wilcox, "Social Movements and Party Politics."

## CHAPTER 3

1. Gilbert, "Minnesota: Battleground Politics in a New Setting"; Gilbert and Peterson, "Minnesota: Onward Quistian Soldiers?"; Gilbert and Peterson, "Minnesota 1998"; Gilbert and Peterson, "Strong Bark, Weak Bite."
2. Engel, *The Unfinished Revolution*.
3. McAdam, *Political Process*; McAdam, McCarthy, and Zald, "Introduction: Opportunities, Mobilizing Structures, and Framing Processes"; Meyer, "Tending the Vineyard."
4. Goldstone, *States, Parties and Social Movements*.
5. Dalton, "Strategies of Partisan Influence"; Kriesi et al., *New Social Movements in Western Europe*.
6. Green and Guth, "Controlling the Mischief of Faction"; Pomper, *Elections in America*.
7. Conger and Green, "Spreading Out and Digging In"; Persinos, "Has the Christian Right Taken Over the Republican Party?"
8. Tarrow, *Power in Movement*, 165.
9. Green, Conger, and Guth, "Christian Right Activist Survey."
10. Wilcox, Jelen, and Linzey, "Rethinking the Reasonableness of the Religious Right."

## CHAPTER 4

1. Smith, "Miller Pitches Himself as Pro-Family, Low-Tax Conservative"; Tully, "In Battle of Endorsements."
2. Callahan, "Rural, Southern, Conservative Voters Key to Daniel's Victory."
3. Tully, "Hoosiers Prefer Faith-Based Officials."

4. Green, *National Survey of Religion and Politics.*
5. Ibid.
6. DeAgostino, "Impasse over Marriage Resolution."
7. Conger, "A Matter of Context."
8. Dillman, "Elkhart at Core of Ten Commandments Fight."
9. LaRaja, "State Parties and Soft Money."
10. Elazar, *American Federalism: A View from the States.*
11. Fenton, *Midwest Politics.*
12. Smith, "Miller Pitches Himself as Pro-Family, Low-Tax Conservative."
13. Pulliam, "Retirement Isn't in His Plans."
14. DeAgostino, "Impasse over Marriage Resolution."
15. Smith, "Republicans Hoping to Force Vote on Gay Marriage Ban."
16. Ibid.

## Chapter 5

1. Green, "National Survey of Religion and Politics."
2. Burnett and Smith, "Missourians and the Political Parties," 64.
3. Mannies, "Past Campaigns in State," B2.
4. Franck and Mannies, "GOP Hopes to Avoid Party Rift."
5. Mannies, "Catholics Will Lobby for Stem Cell Ban," C1.
6. Mannies, "Danforth Gives Views," B2.
7. Mannies, "Bush Visit Spotlights State GOP," A1.
8. Mannies, "GOP Can Flex Its Muscles," E1.
9. Schlozman, Brady, and Verba, "Prospecting for Participants."
10. Mannies, "These Days, Abortion Rights Groups are Kept Scrambling," B2.
11. I and R Institute, "Statewide Initiatives and Referenda."

## Chapter 6

1. Morrison Institute for Public Policy, "Inside How Arizona Compares."
2. Green, "National Survey of Religion and Politics."
3. Uriarte, "Blood Feud."
4. La Raja, "State Parties and Soft Money."
5. Clean Elections Institute, "What Is Clean Elections?"
6. Davenport, "Moderates Form New Political Group."
7. Kelderman, "527's under Scrutiny from States."
8. Rozell and Wilcox, *God at the Grassroots,* 255–56.

9. O'Neil, "Arizona: Pro-Choice Success in a Conservative, Republican State."
10. Crawford, "Supporters of Marriage Amendment Warn Voters."
11. Smith, "Arizona Marriage Amendment Failed."

## CHAPTER 7

1. Green, Rozell, and Wilcox, *Prayers in the Precincts.*
2. Green, "National Survey of Religion and Politics."
3. Conger and Green, "Spreading Out and Digging In."
4. Goodman, "A Vermont Divided by Gay Rights."
5. Conger and McGraw, "The Christian Right and the Requirements of Citizenship."
6. Green, "National Survey of Religion and Politics."

## CHAPTER 8

1. Green, Rozell, and Wilcox, *Prayers in the Precincts*; Green, Rozell, and Wilcox, *Marching to the Millenium*; Green, Roxell, and Wilcox, *The Values Campaign?*; Rozell and Wilcox, *God at the Grassroots*; Rozell and Wilcox, *God at the Grassroots, 1996.*
2. Conger, "Moral Values Issues and Political Party Organizations."
3. Conger and Racheter, "Iowa: In the Heart of Bush Country."
4. Ibid.
5. Green, "Ohio: The Bible and the Buckeye State."
6. Jelen, "Illinois: Moral Politics in a Materialistic Political Culture."
7. Conger, "Party Platforms and Party Coalitions."
8. Bednar and Hertzke, "Oklahoma: The Christian Right and Republican Realignment."
9. Moen and Palmer, "Citizen Initiative in Maine."
10. Wald and Scher, "A Necessary Annoyance?"
11. Conger, "Moral Values Issues and Political Party Organizations."
12. Lunch, "The Christian Right in the Northwest."
13. Conger, "Moral Values Issues and Political Party Organizations."
14. Conger, "A Matter of Context."
15. The seeming discrepancy between a medium level of perceived influence and a going home strategy may have to do with differing definitions of Republican politics. In the influence studies, the ordinal measure of influence was based entirely on the perception of influence in a state's Republican central committee, while the strategy measure was based on a broader picture of Republican politics across the state.

## CHAPTER 9

1. V. O. Key, *American State Politics.*
2. Conger and McGraw, "The Christian Right and the Requirements of Citizenship"; Moen, *The Transformation of the Christian Right*, "The Evolving Politics of the Christian Right."

# BIBLIOGRAPHY

Aldrich, John H. *Why Parties? The Origin and Transformation of Political Parties in America*. Chicago: University of Chicago Press, 1995.

———. "Presidential Address: Southern Parties in State and Nation." *Journal of Politics* 62 (2000): 643–70.

———. "State Political Party Strength." Typescript data provided by investigator, n.d.

Amenta, Edwin. *Bold Relief: Institutional Politics and the Origins of Modern American Social Policy*. Princeton, NJ: Princeton University Press, 1998.

Ansolabehere, Stephen, and Gary King. "Measuring the Consequences of Delegate Selection Rules in Presidential Nominations." *Journal of Politics* 52 (1990): 609–21.

Baer, Denise L., and David A. Bositis. *Elite Cadres and Party Coalitions: Representing the Public in Party Politics*. New York: Greenwood, 1988.

Bates, Vernon L. "The Decline of a New Christian Right Social Movement Organization: Opportunities and Constraints." *Review of Religious Research* 42 (2000): 19–40.

Beck, Paul Allen, and Marjorie Random Hershey. *Party Politics in America*. New York: Longman, 2001.

Bednar, Nancy L., and Allen D. Hertzke. "Oklahoma: The Christian Right and Republican Realignment." In *God at the Grassroots: The Christian Right in the 1994 Elections*, ed. Mark J. Rozell and Clyde Wilcox, 91–107. Lanham, MD: Rowman & Littlefield, 1995.

Bendyna, Mary E., and Clyde Wilcox. "The Christian Right Old and New: A Comparison of the Moral Majority and the Christian Coalition." In *Sojourners in the Wilderness: The Christian Right in Comparative Perspective*, ed. Corwin E. Smidt and James M. Penning, 41–56. Lanham, MD: Rowman & Littlefield, 1997.

Bibby, John F., and Thomas M. Holbrook. "Parties and Elections." In *Politics in the American States: A Comparative Analysis*, ed.

Virginia Gray, Russell L. Hanson, and Herbert Jacob, 66–112. Washington DC: CQ Press, 1999.

Blumenthal, Sidney. "Christian Soldiers." *New Yorker* 70 (1994): 66–112

Bohannon, Mark, Mary Buckley, and David Osborne. *The New Right in the States: The Groups, the Issues, and the Strategies.* Washington DC: Conference on Alternative State and Local Policies, 1984.

Bolce, Louis, and Gerald De Maio. "Our Secularist Democratic Party." *The Public Interest* 149 (2002): 3–20.

Brady, Henry E., Kay Lehman Schlozman, and Sidney Verba. "Prospecting for Participants: Rational Expectations and the Recruitment of Political Activists." *American Political Science Review* 93 (1999): 153–68.

Bruce, Steve. *The Rise and Fall of the New Christian Right.* Oxford, UK: Clarendon, 1988.

Bruce, Steve, Peter Kivisto, and William H. Swatos, Jr. *The Rapture of Politics: The Christian Right as the United States Approaches the year 2000.* New Brunswick, NJ: Transaction, 1995.

"Buchanan Chalks Up Win in Missouri," CNN All Politics, March 9, 1996. http://www.cnn.com/ALLPOLITICS/1996/news/9603/09/missouri.caucus/index.shtml (accessed September 25, 2002).

Burnett, R. E., and Cordell E. Smith. "Missourians and the Political Parties." In *Missouri Government and Politics*, ed. Richard J. Hardy, Richard R. Dohm, and David A. Leuthold, 56–69. Columbia, MO: University of Missouri Press, 1995.

Callahan, Rick. "Rural, Southern, Conservative Voters Key to Daniel's Victory," *Associated Press State and Local Wire*, November 3, 2004.

Capps, Walter H. *The New Religious Right: Piety, Patriotism, And Politics.* Columbia, SC: University of South Carolina Press, 1990.

Carsey, Thomas M., John C. Green, Richard Herrera, and Geoffrey C. Layman. "State Party Context and Norms among Delegates to the 2000 National Party Conventions." *State Politics & Policy Quarterly* 6 (2006): 247–71.

Cavala, William. "Changing the Rules Changes the Game: Party Reform and the 1972 Delegation to the Democratic National Convention." *American Political Science Review* 68 (1974): 27–44.

Clean Elections Institute. "What is Clean Elections?" http://www.azclean.org/about.html (accessed June, 2005).

Cloward, Richard A. and Frances Fox Piven. "Disruptive Dissensus: People and Power in the Industrial Age." In *Reflections on*

*Community Organization*, ed. Jack Rothman, 165–93. Itasca, IL: F. E. Peacock, 1999.

CNN.com. "Election 2000." http:www.cnn.com/ELECTION/2000/ (accessed August, 2000).

Conger, Kimberly H. *Grassroots Activism and Party Politics: The Christian Right in State Republican Parties*. PhD diss., Ohio State University, 2003.

———. "Moral Values Issues and Political Party Organizations: Cycles of Conflict and Accommodation of the Christian Right in State-level Republican Parties." In *The Christian Conservative Movement and American Democracy: Evangelicals, The Religious Right, and American Politics*, ed. Steve Brint and Jean Schroedel. New York: Russell Sage Foundation, forthcoming.

———. "Party Platforms and Party Coalitions: The Christian Right and State Level Republicans." *Party Politics*, forthcoming.

———. "A Matter of Context: Christian Right Influence in State Politics." *State Politics and Policy Quarterly*, forthcoming..

Conger, Kimberly H., and John C. Green. "Spreading Out and Digging In: Christian Conservatives and State Republican Parties." *Campaigns and Elections* 23 (2002): 58–60, 64–65.

Conger, Kimberly H., and Bryan C. McGraw. "The Christian Right and the Requirements of Citizenship: Political Autonomy." *Perspectives on Politics* 6 (2008):253–66.

Conger, Kimberly H., and Donald P. Racheter. "Iowa: In the Heart of Bush Country." In *The Values Campaign? The Christian Right in the 2004 Election*, ed. John C. Green, Mark Rozell, and Clyde Wilcox, 128–42. Washington DC: Georgetown University Press, 2006.

Cooperman, Allan. "Churchgoers Get Direction From Bush Campaign," *Washington Post*, July 1, 2004.

Corrado, Anthony. "The Politics of Cohesion: The Role of the National Party Committees in the 1992 Election." In *The State of the Parties*, ed. John C. Green and Daniel M. Shea, 63–82. Lanham, MD: Rowman & Littlefield, 1996.

Cotter, Cornelius P., James L. Gibson, John F. Bibby, and Robert J. Huckshorn. *Party Organization in American Politics*. New York: Praeger, 1984.

Crawford, Amanda J. "Supporters of marriage amendment warn voters." *Arizona Republican*, October 26, 2006.

Cromartie, Michael. *No Longer Exiles: The Religious New Right in American Politics*. Washington DC: Ethics and Public Policy Center, 1993.

————. *Disciples and Democracy: Religious Conservatives and the Future of American Politics*. Grand Rapids, MI: Eerdmans, 1995.

————. "Religious Conservatives In American Politics 1980–2000: An Assessment." *Witherspoon Fellowship Lectures*. Washington DC: Family Research Council, 2001.

D'Antonio, Michael. "Bedeviling the GOP; With 'Stealth' Candidates, Tight Discipline and Cash, the Religious Right Dominated the Republican Agenda. Now, the Battle's On For the Party's Soul—And Its Future," *LA Times*, November 29, 1992.

Dalton, Russell J. "Strategies of Partisan Influence: West European Environmental Groups." In *The Politics of Social Protest*, ed. J. Craig Jenkins and Bert Klandermans, 296–323. Minneapolis, MN: University of Minnesota Press, 1995.

Dalton, Russell J., and Kuechler, Manfred, ed. *Challenging The Political Order*. Cambridge, MA: Polity, 1990.

Davenport, Paul. "Moderates form new political group." *Associated Press State and Local Wire*, December 10, 2003.

DeAgostino, Martin. "Impasse over marriage resolution; Lack of a quorum stalls all House business for the day," *South Bend Tribune* (Indiana), February 24, 2004.

Deckman, Melissa M. *School Board Battles: The Christian Right in Local Politics*. Washington DC: Georgetown University Press, 2004.

della Porta, Donatella, and Mario Diani. *Social Movements: An Introduction*. Oxford, UK: Blackwell, 1999.

della Porta, Donatella, and Dieter Rucht. "Social Movement Sectors in Context: A Comparison of Italy and West Germany, 1965–1990." In *The Politics of Social Protest*, ed. Craig Jenkins and Bert Klandermans, 229–72. Minneapolis: University of Minnesota Press, 1995.

Diamond, Sara. *Not by Politics Alone: The Enduring Influence of the Christian Right*. New York: Guilford, 1998.

Dillman, Susan. "Elkhart at Core of Ten Commandments Fight." *South Bend Tribune* (Indiana), February 8, 2000.

Djupe, Paul A., and Jacob R. Neiheisel. "Christian Right Horticulture: Grassroots Support in a Republican Primary Campaign." *Politics & Religion* 1 (2008): 55–84.

Downs, Anthony. *An Economic Theory of Democracy*. New York: Longman, 1957.

Edsall, Thomas B. "Robertson Urges Christian Activists to Take Over GOP State Parties," *Washington Post*, September 10, 1995.

Edsall, Thomas B., and David Von Drehle. "Life of the Grand Old Party; Energize Coalition Enters Another Political Phase," *Washington Post*, August 14, 1994.

Eisenstein, Maurice M. *Indiana Politics and Public Policy*. New York: Simon & Schuster, 1999.

Elazar, Daniel. *American Federalism: A View from the States*. New York: Thomas Y. Crowell, 1966.

Eldersveld, Samuel J. *Political Parties in American Society*. New York: Basic Books, 1982.

Eldersveld, Samuel J., and Hanes Walton. *Political Parties in American Society*. Boston: St. Martin's Press, 2000.

Engel, Stephen M. *The Unfinished Revolution: Social Movement Theory and the Gay and Lesbian Movement*. Cambridge, UK: Cambridge University Press, 2001.

———. "Organizational Identity as a Constraint on Strategic Action: A Comparative Analysis of Gay and Lesbian Interest Groups." *Studies in American Political Development* 21 (2007): 66–91.

Engstrom, Erik J., and Samuel Kernell. "Manufactured Responsiveness: The Impact of State Electoral Laws on Unified Party Control of the Presidency and House of Representatives, 1840–1940." *American Journal of Political Science* 49 (2005): 531–49.

Epstein, Leon. *Political Parties in the American Mold*. Madison, WI: University of Wisconsin Press, 1986.

Erikson, Robert S., Gerald C. Wright, and John P. McIver. *Statehouse Democracy: Public Opinion and Policy in the American States*. Cambridge, UK: Cambridge University Press, 1993.

Ewing, Winston. "Freedom's Foundation: Comments from an Ozark Hillbilly." Pamphlet, n.d.

Faith in Public Life. "The Young and the Faithful." October 8, 2008, http://www.faithinpubliclife.org/tools/polls/faps/The%20Young%20and%20the%20Faithful.pdf.

Fenno, Richard F. Jr. *Home Style*. New York: HarperCollins, 1978.

Fenton, John H. *Midwest Politics*. New York: Holt, Rinehart, and Winston, 1996.

Franck, Matthew, and Jo Mannies. "GOP Hopes to Avoid Party Rift in Session Anti-Abortion Measure will be Focus of Work," *St. Louis Post-Dispatch*, September 6, 2005.

Freeman, Jo. "Resource Mobilization and Strategy: A Model for Analyzing Social Movement Organization Actions." In *The Dynamics of Social Movements*, ed. Mayer N. Zald and John D. McCarthy. Cambridge, MA: Winthrop, 1979.

———. "The Political Culture of the Democratic and Republican Parties." *Political Science Quarterly* 101 (1986): 327–56.

George, Alexander L. and Andrew Bennet. *Case Studies and Theory Development in the Social Science.* Cambridge, MA: MIT Press, 2005.

Gerlach, Luther P., and Virginia H. Hine. *People, Power, Change: Movements of Social Transformation.* Indianapolis, IN: Bobbs-Merrill, 1970.

Gilbert, Christopher P. "Minnesota: Battleground Politics in a New Setting." In *The Values Campaign? The Christian Right and the 2004 Elections,* ed. John C. Green, Mark J. Rozell, and Clyde Wilcox, 143–57. Washington DC: Georgetown University Press, 2006.

Gilbert, Christopher P., and David A. M. Peterson. "Minnesota: Onward Quistian Soldiers? Christian Conservatives Confront Their Limitations." In *God at the Grassroots, 1996: The Christian Right in the American Elections,* ed. Mark J. Rozell and Clyde Wilcox, 187–206. Lanham, MA: Rowman & Littlefield, 1997.

———. "Minnesota 1998: Christian Conservatives and the Body Politic." In *Prayers in the Precincts: The Christian Right in the 1998 Elections,* ed. John C. Green, Mark J. Rozell, and Clyde Wilcox, 207–26. Washington DC: Georgetown University Press, 2000.

———. "Strong Bark, Weak Bite: The Strengths and Liabilities of the Christian Right in Minnesota Politics." In *The Christian Right in American Politics: Marching to the Millennium,* ed. John C. Green, Mark J. Rozell, and Clyde Wilcox, 167–86. Washington DC: Georgetown University Press, 2003.

Gimpel, James G. *National Elections and the Autonomy of American State Party Systems.* Pittsburgh: University of Pittsburgh Press, 1996.

Goldstone, Jack A. "Bridging Institutionalized and Noninstitutionalized Politics." In *States, Parties and Social Movements,* ed. Jack A. Goldstone, 1–24. Cambridge, UK: Cambridge University Press, 2003.

———, ed. *States, Parties, and Social Movements.* Cambridge, UK: Cambridge University Press, 2003.

Goodman, Ellen. "A Vermont Divided by Gay Rights," *Times Union,* November 3, 2000.

Gray, Virginia, Russell L. Hanson, and Herbert Jacob. *Politics in the American States: a Comparative Analysis.* Washington DC: CQ Press, 1999.

Green, John C. "National Survey of Religion and Politics." Typescript data provided by investigator, 2000.

———. "Ohio: The Bible and the Buckeye State." In *The Values Campaign: the Christian Right and the 2004 Election,* ed. John C. Green,

Mark J. Rozell, and Clyde Wilcox, 79–97. Washington DC: Georgetown University Press, 2006.

Green, John C., James L. Guth, Corwin E. Smidt, and Lyman A. Kellstedt. *Religion and the Culture Wars: Dispatches from the Front.* New York: Rowman & Littlefield, 1996.

Green, John C., Kimberly H. Conger, and James L. Guth. "Christian Right Activist Survey." Typescript data provided by investigator, 2004.

Green, John C., and James L. Guth. "The Christian Right in the Republican Party: The Case of Pat Robertson's Supporters." *Journal of Politics* 50 (1988): 150–65.

———. "Religion, Representatives, and Roll Calls." *Legislative Studies Quarterly* 16 (1991): 321–44.

———. "Controlling the Mischief of Faction: Party Support and Coalition Building Among Party Activists." In *Politics, Professionalism, and Power: Modern Party Organization and the Legacy of Ray C. Bliss*, ed. John C. Green, 234–64. Lanham, MD: University Press of America, 1994.

Green, John C., James L. Guth, and Kevin Hill. "Faith and Election: The Christian Right in Congressional Campaigns 1978–88." *Journal of Politics* 55 (1993): 80–91.

Green, John C., James L. Guth, and Clyde Wilcox. "Less than Conquerors: The Christian Right in State Republican Parties." In *Social Movements and American Political Institutions*, ed. Anne N. Costain and Andrew S. McFarland, 117–35. Lanham, MD: Rowman & Littlefield, 1998.

Green, John C., Mark J. Rozell, and Clyde Wilcox. *Prayers in the Precincts: The Christian Right in the 1998 Elections.* Washington DC: Georgetown University Press, 2000.

———. "Social Movements and Party Politics: The Case of the Christian Right." *Journal for the Scientific Study of Religion* 40 (2001): 413–26.

———. *The Christian Right in American Politics: Marching to the Millennium.* Washington DC: Georgetown University Press, 2003.

———. *The Values Campaign?: The Christian Right and the 2004 Elections.* Washington DC: Georgetown University Press, 2006.

Gusfield, Joseph R. *Protest, Reform and Revolt: A Reader in Social Movements.* New York: John Wiley & Sons, 1970.

Guth, James. "The Politics of the Christian Right?" In *Interest Group Politics*, ed. Allan Ciglar and Burdett Loomis, 60–83. Washington DC: CQ Press, 1983.

Hacker, Hans J. *The Culture of Conservative Christian Litigation.* Lanham, MD: Rowman & Littlefield, 2005.

Hadley, David. J. 1997. "Indiana." In *State Party Profiles: A 50-state guide to development, organization, and resources,* ed. Andrew M. Appleton and Daniel S. Ward, 95–102. Washington DC: CQ Press, 1997.

Hardy, Richard J., Richard R. Dohm, and David A. Leuthold. *Missouri Politics and Government.* Columbia, MO: University of Missouri Press, 1995.

Herman, Ken. "GOP Politics: A Religious Experience," *Austin American Statesman,* June 5, 2004.

Hertzke, Allen D. *Representing God in Washington: The Role of Religious Lobbies in the American Polity.* Knoxville, TN: University of Tennessee Press, 1988.

———. *Echoes of Discontent: Jesse Jackson, Pat Robertson, and the Resurgence of Populism.* Washington DC: CQ Press, 1993.

Hofrenning, Daniel. *In Washington but Not of It.* Philadelphia, PA: Temple University Press, 1995.

Hogan, Robert E. "State Campaign Finance Laws and Interest Group Electioneering Activities." *The Journal of Politics* 67 (2005): 887–906.

Initiative and Referendum Institute. "Statewide Initiatives and Referenda," http://www.iandrinstitute.org/statewide-i&r.htm (accessed May, 2006).

IN.gov. State of Indiana Web site. http://www.in.gov.

Jelen, Ted G. "Citizenship, Discipleship, and Democracy: Evaluating the Impact of the Christian Right." In *Sojourners in the Wilderness: The Christian Right in Comparative Perspective,* ed. Corwin E. Smidt and James M. Penning, 249–68. Lanham, MA: Rowman & Littlefield, 1997.

———. "Illinois: Moral Politics in a Materialistic Political Culture." In *Prayers in the Precincts: the Christian Right in the 1998 Elections,* ed. Mark J. Rozell and Clyde Wilcox, 243–55. Washington DC: Georgetown University Press, 2000.

Jenkins, J. Craig, and Bert Klandermans, ed. *The Politics of Protest: Comparative Perspectives on States and Social Movements.* Minneapolis, MN: University of Minnesota Press, 1995.

Jewell, Malcolm E., and Sarah M. Morehouse. *Political Parties and Elections in American States.* Washington DC: CQ Press, 2001.

Jewell, Malcolm E., and David M. Olson. *Political Parties and Elections in American States.* Washington DC: CQ Press, 1982, 1988.

Jorstad, Erling. *The New Christian Right 1981–1988: Prospects for the Post Reagan Decade*. Lewiston, NY: Edwin Mellen, 1987.

Kelderman, Eric. "527's Under Scrutiny from States." October 26, 2005. http://www.stateline.org/live/ViewPage.action?siteNodeId=136&languageId=1&contentId=63077 (accessed June 5, 2007).

Key, V. O. *American State Politics: An Introduction*. New York: Knopf, 1956.

King, Gary, Robert O. Keohane, and Sidney Verba. *Designing Social Inquiry: Scientific Inference in Qualitative Research*. Princeton, NJ: Princeton University Press, 1994.

Kitschelt, Herbert. "Political Opportunity Structure and Political Protest: Anti-Nuclear Movements in Four Democracies." *British Journal of Political Science* 16 (1986): 57–85.

———. *The Logics of Party Formation: Ecological Politics in Belgium and West Germany*. Ithaca, NY: Cornell University Press, 1989.

Klandermans, Bert, Hanspeter Kriesi, and Sidney Tarrow, eds. *From Structure to Action*. Greenwich, CT: JAI, 1988.

Kriesi, Hanspeter, Ruud Koopmans, Jan Willem Dyvendak, and Marco G. Giugni. *New Social Movements in Western Europe: A Comparative Analysis*. Minneapolis, MN: University of Minnesota Press, 1995.

Kubik, Jan. "Institutionalization of Protest during Democratic Consolidation in Central Europe." In *The Social Movement Society: Contentious Politics for a New Century*, ed. David S. Meyer and Sidney Tarrow, 131–52. Lanham, MD: Rowman & Littlefield, 1998.

La Raja, Raymond J. "State Parties and Soft Money: How Much Party Building?" In *The State of Parties: 2000 and Beyond*, ed. John C. Green, 132–50. New York: Rowman & Littlefield, 2003.

Leege, David C., and Lyman A. Kellstedt. *Rediscovering the Religious Factor in American Politics*. Armonk, NY: M. E. Sharpe, 1993.

Liebman, Robert C., and Robert Wuthnow. *The New Christian Right: Mobilization and Legitimation*. Hawthorne, NY: Aldine, 1983.

Lienesch, Michael. *Redeeming America: Piety and Politics in the New Christian Right*. Chapel Hill, NC: University of North Carolina Press, 1993.

———. *In the Beginning: Fundamentalism, the Scopes Trial, and the Making of the Antievolution Movement*. Chapel Hill, NC: University of North Carolina Press, 2007.

Lo, Clarence Y. H. "Countermovements and Conservative Movements in the Contemporary U.S." *Annual Review of Sociology* 8 (1982): 107–34.

Lunch, William M. "The Christian Right in the Northwest: Two Decades of Frustration in Oregon and Washington." In *The Christian Right in American Politics: Marching to the Millennium*, ed. John C. Green, Mark J. Rozell, and Clyde Wilcox, 231–53. Washington DC: Georgetown University Press, 2003.

Madison, James H. *The Indiana Way: A State History*. Bloomington, IN: Indiana University Press, 1986.

Maguire, Diarmuid. "Opposition Movements and Opposition Parties: Equal Partners of Dependent Relations in the Struggle for Power and Reform." In *The Politics of Social Protest*, ed. Craig J. Jenkins and Bert Klandermans, 199–228. Minneapolis, MN: University of Minnesota Press, 1995.

Mannies, Jo. "Missouri GOP Adopts New Platform at Convention." *St. Louis Post-Dispatch*, June 18, 2000.

———. "GOP can Flex its Muscle near Springfield." *St. Louis Post-Dispatch*, September 12, 2004.

———. "Past Campaigns in State Show Peril of Relying Solely on Polls," *St. Louis Post-Dispatch*, September 13, 2004.

———. "Catholics will Lobby for Stem-Cell Ban," *St. Louis Post-Dispatch*, April 1, 2005.

———. "Bush Visit Spotlights State GOP: The President Will Find that Missouri Republicans' Fortunes Seem to Mirror Those of the National Party," *St. Louis Post-Dispatch*, May 31, 2005.

———. "Danforth Gives Views on Gay Issue," *St. Louis Post-Dispatch*, August 26, 2005.

———. "These Days, Abortion Rights Groups are Kept Scrambling," *St. Louis Post-Dispatch*, September 5, 2005.

Martin, William. *With God on Our Side: The Rise of the Religious Right in America*. New York: Broadway Books, 1996.

May, Lee. "Robertson Exhorts Followers to Run for Local Offices," *Los Angeles Times*, March 7, 1988.

McAdam, Doug. *Political Process and the Development of Black Insurgency 1930–1970*. Chicago, IL: University of Chicago Press, 1982.

McAdam, Doug, John D. McCarthy, and Mayer N. Zald. "Introduction: Opportunities, Mobilizing Structures, and Framing Processes-Toward a Synthetic, Comparative Perspective on Social Movements." In *Comparative Perspectives on Social Movements*, ed. Doug McAdarn, John D. McCarthy and Mayer N. Zald, 1–22. New York: Cambridge University Press, 1996.

McCarthy, John D., and Mayer Zald. "Resource Mobilization and Social Movements: A Partial Theory." In *Social Movements in an*

*Organizational Society*, ed. Mayer N. Zald and John D. McCarthy, 15–42. New Brunswick, NJ: Transaction Books, 1987.

Meyer, David S. "Tending the Vineyard: Cultivating Political Process Research." *Sociological Forum* (1999): 79–92.

Meyer, Joyce. Address. 2002 Christian Coalition Road to Victory Conference. Washington DC, October 11, 2002.

Missouri.gov. Missouri State Government Web site. http://www.missouri.gov.

Moen, Matthew C. *The Transformation of the Christian Right.* Tuscaloosa, AL: University of Alabama Press, 1992.

———. "The Evolving Politics of the Christian Right." *PS: Political Science and Politics* 29 (1996): 461–64.

Moen, Matthew C., and Kenneth T. Palmer. "Citizen Initiative in Maine." In *The Christian Right in American Politics: Marching to the Millennium,* ed. John C. Green, Mark J. Rozell, and Clyde Wilcox, 255–76. Washington DC: Georgetown University Press, 2003.

Monroe, J. P. *The Political Party Matrix: The Persistence of Organization.* Albany, NY: State University of New York Press, 2001.

Morrison Institute for Public Policy. "Inside How Arizona Compares: Getting the Real Numbers." Pamphlet, 2005.

Müller, Wolfgang C., and Kaare Strøm. "Party Behavior and Representative Democracy." In *Policy, Office, or Votes? How Political Parties in Western Europe Make Hard Decisions,* ed. Wolfgang C. Müller and Kaare Strøm, 279–310. Cambridge, UK: Cambridge University Press, 1999.

Mydans, Seth. "Christian Conservatives Counting Hundreds of Gains in Local Votes," *New York Times,* November 21, 1992.

Neuhaus, Richard John, and Michael Cromartie. *Piety and Policy: Evangelicals and Fundamentalists Confront the World.* Washington DC: Ethics and Public Policy Center, 1987.

North, Douglass C. "Economic Performance Through Time." *American Economic Review* 84 (1994): 359–68.

OED Online. "Influence." http://dictionary.oed.com/cgi/entry/00116447 (accessed September 17, 2001).

Oldfield, Duane Murray. *The Right and the Righteous: The Christian Right Confronts the Republican Party.* Lanham, MD: Rowman & Littlefield, 1996.

Olson, Mancur. *The Logic of Collective Action: Public Goods and the Theory of Groups.* Cambridge, MA: Harvard University Press, 1965.

O'Neil, Daniel J. "Arizona: Pro-Choice Success in a Conservative, Republican State," In *Abortion Politics in American States.* ed.

Timothy A. Byrnes and Mary C. Segers, 85–101. Armonk, NY: M. E. Sharpe, 1995.

Paddock, Joel. "Missouri." In *State Party Profiles: A 50-State Guide to Development, Organization, and Resources*, ed. Andrew M. Appleton and Daniel S. Ward, 177–84. Washington DC: CQ Press, 1997.

Penning, James M. "Pat Robertson and the GOP: 1988 and Beyond." *Sociology of Religion* 55 (1994): 327–44.

Persinos, John F. "Has the Christian Right Taken Over the Republican Party?" *Campaigns and Elections* 15 (1994): 20–24.

Pew Forum on Religion and Public Life. "A Post-Election Look at Religious Voters in the 2008 Election." http://www.pewforum.org/events/?EventID=209 (accessed December 8, 2008).

Piven, Frances Fox, and Richard A. Cloward. *Poor People's Movements: Why They Succeed, How They Fail.* New York: Vintage Books, 1979.

Pomper, Gerald M. *Elections in America: Control and Influence in Democratic Politics.* New York: Dodd, Mead, 1976.

Pulliam, Russ. "Retirement Isn't in his Plans," *Indianapolis Star*, 25 September 2005.

Racheter, Donald R., Lyman A. Kellstedt, and John C. Green. "Iowa: Crucible of the Christian Right." In *The Christian Right in American Politics: Marching to the Millennium*, ed. John C. Green, Mark J. Rozell, and Clyde Wilcox, 121–44. Washington DC: Georgetown University Press, 2002.

Reed, Ralph. *Politically Incorrect.* Dallas, TX: Word Publishing, 1994.

———. *Active Faith.* New York: Free Press, 1996.

Reichley, A. James. *The Life of the Parties: A History of American Political Parties.* Lanham, MD: Rowman & Littlefield, 1992.

Rossiter, Clinton. *Parties and Politics in America*: Ithaca, NY: Cornell University Press, 1960.

Rozell, Mark J., and Clyde Wilcox. *God at the Gross Roots: The Christian Right in the 1994 Elections.* Lanham, MD: Rowman & Littlefield, 1995.

———. *Second Coming: The New Christian Right in Virginia Politics.* Baltimore, MD: Johns Hopkins University Press, 1996.

———. *God at the Grass Roots, 1996: The Christian Right in the American Elections.* Lanham, MD: Rowman & Littlefield, 1997.

Rucht, Dieter. "The Strategies and Action Repertoires of New Movements." In *Challenging the Political Order*, ed. Russell J. Dalton and Manfred Kuechler, 156–75. Cambridge, UK: Polity Press, 1990.

Schlafly, Phyllis. "ERA Mischief in Missouri." February 14, 2001. http://www.eagleforum.org/era/2001/Era-mo-2001.shtml (accessed June 15, 2001).

Schlesinger, Joseph A. *Political Parties and the Winning of Office.* Ann Arbor, MI: University of Michigan Press, 1991.

Schlozman, Kay Lehman, Henry E. Brady, and Sidney Verba. "Prospecting for Participants: Rational Expectations and the Recruitment of Political Activists." *American Political Science Review* 93 (1999): 153–68.

Smidt, Corwin E., and James M. Penning. *Sojourners in the Wilderness: The Christian Right in Comparative Perspective.* Lanham, MA: Rowman & Littlefield, 1997.

Smith, Christian. *Christian America? What Evangelicals Really Want.* Berkeley, CA: University of California Press, 2000.

Smith, Gregory A. "Do the Democrats Have a God Problem? How Public Perceptions May Spell Trouble for the Party." *Pew Forum on Religion and Public Life Survey Report.* http://pewforum.org/docs/index.php?DocID=148 (2006).

Smith, Mike. "Majority of House Members Support Ban on Same-Sex Marriage," *Associated Press State and Local Wire*, January 29, 2004.

———. "Miller Pitches himself as Pro-Family, Low-Tax Conservative," *Indianapolis Star*, April 27, 2004.

———. "Republicans Hoping to Force Vote on Gay Marriage Ban," *Associated Press State and Local Wire*, February 23, 2004.

Smith, Peter J. "Arizona Marriage Amendment Failed Because it Also Affected Unwed Heterosexuals." November 24, 2006. http://www.lifesite.net/Idn/2006/nov/06112411.html

Soule, Sarah A., and Susan Olzak. "When Do Movements Matter? The Politics of Contingency and the Equal Rights Amendment." *American Sociological Review* 69 (2004): 473–97.

Sundquist, James L. *Dynamics of the Party System: Alignment and Realignment of Political Parties in the United States.* Washington DC: Brookings Institution, 1983.

Tansey, Oisin. "Process-Tracing and Elite Interviewing: A Case for Non-Probability Sampling." *PS: Political Science & Politics* 40 (2007): 765–72.

Tarrow, Sidney. "Social Movements in Contentious Politics: A Review Article." *American Political Science Review* 90 (1996): 874–83.

———. *Power in Movement: Social Movements and Contentious Politics.* New York: Cambridge University Press, 1998.

———. "Paradigm Warriors: Regress and Progress in the Study of Contentious Politics." *Sociological Forum* 14 (1999): 71–77.

Thomas, Cal, and Ed Dobson. *Blinded By Might: Can the Religious Right Save America?* Grand Rapids, MI: Zondervan, 1999.

Tully, Matthew. "In Battle of Endorsements, Miller gets Bowen's Nod," *Indianapolis Star*, March 10, 2004. http://www.Indystar .com (accessed March 10, 2004).

———. "Hoosiers prefer faith-based officials," *Indianapolis Star*, June 28, 2004, City Edition.

Uriarte, Richard de. "Blood Feud," *Arizona Republic*, September 5, 2004.

Urofsky, Melvin I., and Martha May. *New Christian Right: Political and Social Issues*. New York: Garland, 1996.

Usher, Douglas. "Strategy, Rules and Participation: Issue Activists in Republican National Convention Delegations, 1976–1996." *Political Research Quarterly* 53 (2000): 887–903.

Verba, Sidney, Kay Lehman Schlozman, and Henry E. Brady. *Voice and Equality: Civic Voluntarism in American Politics*. Cambridge, MA: Harvard University Press, 1995.

Wald, Kenneth D. *Religion and Politics in the United States*. Washington DC: CQ Press, 1997.

Wald, Kenneth D., and Jeffrey C. Corey. "The Christian Right and Public Policy: Social Movement Elites as Institutional Activists." *State Politics and Policy Quarterly* 2 (2002): 99–125.

Wald, Kenneth D., and Richard K. Scher. "'A Necessary Annoyance'? The Christian Right and the Development of Republican Party Politics in Florida." In *The Christian Right in American Politics: Marching to the Millennium*, ed. John C. Green, Mark J. Rozell, and Clyde Wilcox, 79–100. Washington DC: Georgetown University Press, 2003.

Wald, Kenneth D., Adam L. Silverman, and Kevin S. Fridy. "Making Sense of Religion in Political Life." *Annual Review of Political Science* 8 (2005): 121–43

Watson, Justin. *The Christian Coalition: Dreams of Restoration, Demands for Recognition*. New York: St. Martin's Press, 1997.

Weber, Ronald E., and Paul Brace. *American State and Local Politics: Directions for the 21st Century*. New York: Chatham, 1999.

Wilcox, Clyde. *God's Warriors: The Christian Right in Twentieth Century America*. Baltimore, MD: Johns Hopkins University Press, 1992.

———. *Onward Christian Soldiers? The Religious Right in American Politics*. Boulder, CO: Westview, 1996, 2000.

Wilcox, Clyde, Ted G. Jelen, and Sharon Linzey. "Rethinking the Reasonableness of the Religious Right." *Review of Religious Research* 36 (1995): 263–76.

Wilson, James Q. *Political Organizations*. Princeton, NJ: Princeton University Press, 1973, 1995.

# INDEX